AIRMONT SHAKESPEARE CLASSICS SERIES

A
Midsummer
Night's Dream

By

William
Shakespeare

AIRMONT PUBLISHING COMPANY, INC.
22 EAST 60TH STREET · NEW YORK 10022

PUBLISHED SIMULTANEOUSLY IN THE DOMINION OF CANADA
BY THE RYERSON PRESS, TORONTO

PRINTED IN THE UNITED STATES OF AMERICA
BY THE COLONIAL PRESS INC., CLINTON, MASSACHUSETTS

PREFACE

For the Airmont series of plays by William Shakespeare, we have chosen a text that we believe more nearly preserves the flavor of the old Shakespearean English than do those of more modernized versions.

In a popular-priced paperback edition, it is almost impossible to include a complete compilation of notes because of the limitations of the format. We suggest that the reader refer to the following excellent textbooks for additional material: The New Valiorum (Cambridge and Arden editions); the Globe edition edited by W. G. Clark and W. A. Wright (1866); the Oxford edition edited by W. J. Craig (1891); and the editions by G. L. Kittredge (1936). Also, the following books will be helpful to a better understanding of Shakespeare: Harley Granville-Barker, *Prefaces to Shakespeare, First Series* (London, 1933); Gerald Sanders, *A Shakespeare Primer* (New York and Toronto, 1945); J. Dover Wilson, The Essential Shakespeare (London, 1930).

Dr. David G. Pitt received his B.A. degree from Mt. Allison University in New Brunswick, and his M.A. and Ph.D. degrees from the University of Toronto. Since 1949, he has been in the English Department of Memorial University of Newfoundland and Professor of English there since 1962. His publications include articles on literary and educational subjects, and editorial work on Shakespeare.

GENERAL INTRODUCTION

William Shakespeare: His Life, Times, and Theatre

HIS LIFE

The world's greatest poet and playwright, often called the greatest Englishman, was born in Stratford-on-Avon, Warwickshire, in the year 1564. The exact date of his birth is uncertain, but an entry in the *Stratford Parish Register* gives his baptismal date as April 26. Since children were usually baptized two or three days after birth, it is reasonable to assume that he was born on or about April 23—an appropriate day, being the feast of St. George, the patron saint of England.

His father, John Shakespeare, was a glover and dealer in wool and farm products, who had moved to Stratford from Snitterfield, four miles distant, some time before 1552. During his early years in Stratford his business prospered, enabling him to acquire substantial property, including several houses, and to take his place among the more considerable citizens of the town. In 1557 he married Mary, daughter of Robert Arden, a wealthy landowner of Wilmcote, not far from Stratford. Two daughters were born to them before William's birth—Joan, baptized in 1558, and Margaret, baptized in 1562—but both died in infancy. William was thus their third child, though the eldest of those who survived infancy. After him were born Gilbert (1566), another Joan (1569), Anne (1571), Richard (1574), and Edmund (1580).

Very little is positively known (though much is conjectured) about Shakespeare's boyhood and education. We know that for some years after William's birth his father's rise in Stratford society and municipal affairs continued. Many local offices came to him in rapid succession: ale-taster, burgess (a kind of constable), assessor of fines, chamberlain (town treasurer), high bailiff (a kind of magistrate), alderman (town councilor), and chief alderman in 1571. As the son of a man of such eminence in Stratford, Shakespeare undoubtedly attended the local Grammar School. This he was entitled to do free of charge, his father being a town councilor. No records of the school are extant, so that we do not know how good a pupil he was nor what subjects he studied. It is probable that he covered the usual Elizabethan curriculum: an "A B C book," the catechism in Latin and English, Latin grammar, the translation of Latin authors, and perhaps some Greek grammar and translation as well. But family circumstances appear to have curtailed his formal education before it was complete, for shortly before William reached his fourteenth birthday his father's rising fortunes abruptly passed their zenith.

Although we do not know all the facts, it is apparent that about the year 1578, having gone heavily into debt, John Shakespeare lost two large farms inherited by his wife from her father. Thereafter, he was involved in a series of lawsuits, and lost his post on the Stratford town council. Matters got steadily worse for him, until finally in 1586 he was declared a bankrupt. But by this time the future poet-dramatist was already a family man himself.

In 1582, in the midst of his father's legal and financial crises —and perhaps because of them—Shakespeare married Anne, daughter of Richard Hathaway (recently deceased) of the village of Shottery near Stratford. The *Episcopal Register* for the Diocese of Worcester contains their marriage record, dated November 28, 1582; he was then in his eighteenth year and his wife in her twenty-sixth. On May 26 of the following year the *Stratford Parish Register* recorded the baptism of their first child, Susanna; and on February 2, 1585, the baptism of a twin son and daughter named Hamnet and Judith.

These facts are all that are known of Shakespeare's early life. How he supported his family, whether he took up some trade or profession, how long he continued to live in Stratford, we do not know for certain. Tradition and conjecture have bestowed on him many interim occupations between his marriage and his appearance in London in the early fifteen-nineties: printer, dyer, traveling-player, butcher, soldier, apothecary, thief—it reads like a children's augury-rhyme (when buttons or cherrystones are read to learn one's fate). Perhaps only the last-named "pursuit" requires some explanation. According to several accounts, one of them appearing in the first *Life* of Shakespeare by Nicholas Rowe (1709), Shakespeare fell into bad company some time after his marriage, and on several occasions stole deer from the park of Sir Thomas Lucy, a substantial gentleman of Charlecote, near Stratford. According to Rowe:

> For this he was prosecuted by that gentleman, as he thought somewhat too severely; and in order to revenge that ill-usage, he made a ballad upon him . . . and was obliged to leave his business and family in Warwickshire, for some time, and shelter himself in London.

The story has been repeated in varying forms by most subsequent biographers, but its authenticity is doubted by many who repeat it.

Another much more attractive story, which, however, if true, does not necessarily deny the authenticity of Rowe's, is that

Shakespeare during the so-called "lost years" was a school-master. This, indeed, appears to be somewhat better substantiated. John Aubrey, seventeenth-century biographer and anti-quary, in his *Brief Lives* (1681) declares that he had learned from a theatrical manager, whose father had known Shake-speare, that the dramatist "had been in his younger years a schoolmaster in the country." This may, then, account, in part at least, for the years between his marriage and his arrival in London about the year 1591. It is interesting to note that in two of his early plays Shakespeare includes a schoolmaster among his characters: Holofernes of *Love's Labour's Lost* and Pinch of *The Comedy of Errors*. But let us hope that neither is intended to be Shakespeare's portrait of himself.

However he may have occupied himself in the interim, we know that by 1592 he was already a budding actor and play-wright in London. In that year Robert Greene in his autobio-graphical pamphlet *A Groatsworth of Wit*, referring to the young actors and menders of old plays who were, it seemed to him, gaining undeserved glory from the labours of their betters (both by acting their plays and by rewriting them), wrote as follows:

> Yes trust them not: for there is an upstart Crow, beautified with our feathers, that with his Tygers heart wrapt in a Play-ers hyde, supposes he is as well able to bombast out blanke verse as the best of you: and being an absolute *Johannes fac-totum*, is in his owne conceit the onely Shakescene in a countrey.

"Shakescene" is clearly Shakespeare. The phrase "upstart Crow" probably refers to his country origins and his lack of uni-versity education. "Beautified with our feathers" probably means that he uses the older playwrights' words for his own aggrandisement either in plays in which he acts or in those he writes himself. "Tygers heart wrapt in a Players hyde" is a parody of a line of III *Henry VI*, one of the earliest plays ascribed to Shakespeare. And the Latin phrase *Johannes fac-totum*, meaning Jack-of-all-trades, suggests that he was at this time engaged in all sorts of theatrical jobs: actor, poet, play-wright, and perhaps manager as well.

Greene died shortly after making this scurrilous attack on the young upstart from Stratford, and so escaped the resent-ment of those he had insulted. But Henry Chettle, himself a minor dramatist, who had prepared Greene's manuscript for the printer, in his *Kind-Harts Dreame* (1592), apologized to Shakespeare for his share in the offence:

> I am as sory as if the originall fault had beene my fault, be-cause my selfe have seene his demeanor no lesse civill, than he excelent in the qualitie he professes: Besides, divers of

worship have reported his uprightness of dealing, which argues honesty, and his facetious grace in writing, that approoves his Art.

Thus, in a very indirect manner and because of an attack upon him by an irascible dying man, we learn that Shakespeare at this time was in fact held in high regard by "divers of worship," that is, by many of high birth, as an upright, honest young man of pleasant manners and manifest skill as actor, poet, and playwright.

Although Shakespeare by 1593 had written, or written parts of, some five or six plays (I, II, and III *Henry VI, Richard III, The Comedy of Errors,* and perhaps *Titus Andronicus*), it was as a non-dramatic poet that he first appeared in print. *Venus and Adonis* and *The Rape of Lucrece,* long narrative poems, both bearing Shakespeare's name, were published in 1593 and 1594 respectively. But thereafter for the next twenty years he wrote almost nothing but drama. In his early period, 1591 to 1596, in addition to the plays named above, he wrote *Love's Labour's Lost, The Taming of the Shrew, Two Gentlemen of Verona, Romeo and Juliet, A Midsummer Night's Dream, Richard II,* and *King John.* Then followed his great middle period, 1596 to 1600, during which he wrote both comedies and history-plays: *The Merchant of Venice, I* and *II Henry IV, The Merry Wives of Windsor, Much Ado about Nothing, Henry V, Julius Caesar, As You Like It,* and *Twelfth Night.* The period of his great tragedies and the so-called "dark comedies" followed (1600-1608): *Hamlet, Troilus and Cressida, All's Well that Ends Well, Measure for Measure, Othello, King Lear, Macbeth, Antony and Cleopatra, Timon of Athens,* and *Coriolanus.* The last phase of his career as dramatist, 1608 to 1613, sometimes called "the period of the romances," produced *Pericles, Prince of Tyre, Cymbeline, The Winter's Tale, The Tempest,* parts of *Henry VIII,* and perhaps parts of *The Two Noble Kinsmen.* Many other plays were ascribed to him, but it is doubtful that he had a hand in any but those we have named. Long before his death in 1616 his name held such magic for the public that merely to print it on the title page of any play assured its popular acclaim. The "upstart Crow" had come a long way since 1592.

He had come a long way too from the economic straits that may well have driven him to London many years before. We know, for example, from the records of tax assessments that by 1596 Shakespeare was already fairly well-to-do. This is further borne out by his purchasing in the following year a substantial house known as New Place and an acre of land in Stratford for £60, a sizable sum in those days. In 1602 he made a further purchase of 107 acres at Stratford for £320 and a cottage and more land behind his estate at New Place. But his life during this time was not quite unclouded. His only son, Hamnet, died in 1596 at the age of eleven years, his father in 1601, and his mother in 1608. All three were buried in Stratford. More happily he saw, in 1607, the marriage of his daughter Susanna to Dr. John Hall, an eminent physician of Stratford, and in the following year, the baptism of his granddaughter, Elizabeth Hall.

Shakespeare's retirement to Stratford appears to have been gradual, but by 1613, if not earlier, he seems to have settled there, though he still went up to London occasionally. Of the last months of his life we know little. We do know that in February, 1616, his second daughter, Judith, married Thomas Quiney. We know that on March 25, apparently already ill, Shakespeare revised and signed his will, among other bequests leaving to his wife his "second best bed with the furniture." A month later he was dead, dying on his fifty-second birthday, April 23, 1616. He was buried in the chancel of Holy Trinity Church, Stratford, on April 26.

HIS TIMES

Shakespeare lived during the English Renaissance, that age of transition that links the Mediævil and the Modern world. Inheriting the rich traditions of the Middle Ages in art, learning, religion, and politics, rediscovering the great legacies of classical culture, the men of the Renaissance went on to new and magnificent achievements in every phase of human endeavour. No other period in history saw such varied and prolific development and expansion. And the reign of Elizabeth I (1558-1603), Shakespeare's age, was the High Renaissance in England.

Development and expansion—these are the watchwords of the age, and they apply to every aspect of life, thought, and activity. The universe grew in immensity as men gradually abandoned the old Ptolemaic view of a finite, earth-centered universe, accepting the enormous intellectual challenge of the illimitable cosmos of Copernicus' theory and Galileo's telescope. The earth enlarged, too, as more of its surface was discovered and charted by explorers following the lead of Columbus, Cabot, Magellan, and Vespucci. England itself expanded as explorers and colonizers, such as Frobisher, Davis, Gilbert, Raleigh, Grenville, Drake, and others, carried the English flag into many distant lands and seas; as English trade and commerce expanded with the opening of new markets and new sources of supply; as English sea power grew to protect the trading routes and fend off rivals, particularly Spain, the defeat of whose Invincible Armada in 1588 greatly advanced English national pride at home, and power and prestige abroad.

The world of ideas changed and expanded, too. The rediscovery and reinterpretation of the classics, with their broad and humane view of life, gave a new direction and impetus to secular education. During the Middle Ages theology had dominated education, but now the language, literature, and philosophy of the ancient world, the practical arts of grammar, logic, and rhetoric, and training in morals, manners, and gymnastics assumed the major roles in both school and university—in other words, an education that fitted one for life in the world here and now replaced one that looked rather to the life hereafter. Not that the spiritual culture of man was neglected. Indeed, it took on a new significance, for as life in this world acquired new meaning and value, religion assumed new functions, and new vitality to perform them, as the bond between the Creator and a new kind of creation.

It was, of course, the old creation—man and nature—but it was undergoing great changes. Some of these we have already seen, but the greatest was in man's conception of himself and his place in nature. The Mediæval view of man was generally not an exalted one. It saw him as more or less depraved, fallen from Grace as a result of Adam's sin; and the things of this world, which was also "fallen," as of little value in terms of his salvation. Natural life was thought of mainly as a preparation for man's entry into Eternity. But Renaissance thought soon began to rehabilitate man, nature, and the things of this life. Without denying man's need for Grace and the value of the means of salvation provided by the Church, men came gradually to accept the idea that there were "goods", values, "innocent delights" to be had in the world here and now, and that God had given them for man to enjoy. Man himself was seen no longer as wholly vile and depraved, incapable even of desiring goodness, but rather as Shakespeare saw him in *Hamlet*:

What a piece of work is man! how noble in reason! how infinite in faculty! in form and moving how express and admirable! in action how like an angel! in apprehension how like a god! the beauty of the world! the paragon of animals!

And this is the conception of man that permeates Elizabethan thought and literature. It does not mean that man is incorruptible, immune to moral weakness and folly. Shakespeare has his villains, cowards, and fools. But man is none of these by nature; they are distortions of the true form of man. Nature framed him for greatness, endowed him with vast capacities for knowledge, achievement, and delight, and with aspirations that may take him to the stars. "O brave new world, That has such people in 't!"

The chief object of man's aspiring mind is now the natural world, whose "wondrous architecture," says Marlowe's *Tam-*

burlaine, our souls strive ceaselessly to comprehend, "Still climbing after knowledge infinite." Hamlet, too, speaks of "this goodly frame, the earth . . . this brave o'erhanging firmament, this majestical roof fretted with golden fire." No longer the ruins of a fallen paradise and the devil's, nature is seen as man's to possess, her beauty and wonder to be sought after and enjoyed, her energies to be controlled and used—as Bacon expressed it, "for the glory of the Creator and the relief of man's estate."

It was, indeed, a very stirring time to be alive in. New vistas were breaking upon the human mind and imagination everywhere. It was a time like spring, when promise, opportunity, challenge and growth appeared where none had been dreamed of before. Perhaps this is why there is so much poetry of springtime in the age of Shakespeare.

HIS THEATRE

There were many theatres, or playhouses, in Shakespeare's London. The first was built in 1576 by James Burbage and was called the *Theater.* It was built like an arena, with a movable platform at one end, and had no seats in the pit, but had benches in the galleries that surrounded it. It was built of wood, and cost about £200. Other famous playhouses of Shakespeare's time, for the most part similarly constructed, included the Curtain, the Bull, the Rose, the Swan, the Fortune, and, most famous of them all, the Globe. It was built in 1599 by the sons of James Burbage, and it was here that most of Shakespeare's plays were performed. Since more is known about the Globe than most of the others, I shall use it as the basis of the brief account that follows of the Elizabethan playhouse.

As its name suggests, the Globe was a circular structure (the second Globe, built in 1614 after the first burned down, was octagonal), and was open to the sky, somewhat like a modern football or baseball stadium, though much smaller. It had three tiers of galleries surrounding the central "yard" or pit, and a narrow roof over the top gallery. But most interesting from our viewpoint was the stage—or rather *stages*—which was very different from that of most modern theatres. These have the familiar "picture-frame" stage: a raised platform at one end of the auditorium, framed by curtains and footlights, and viewed only from the front like a picture. Shakespeare's stage was very different.

The main stage, or *apron* as it was called, jutted well out into the pit, and did not extend all the way across from side to side. There was an area on either side for patrons to sit or stand in, so that actors performing on the apron could be viewed from three sides instead of one. In addition there was an inner stage, a narrow rectangular recess let into the wall behind the main stage. When not in use it could be closed by a curtain drawn across in front; when open it could be used for interior scenes, arbor scenes, tomb and anteroom scenes and the like. On either side of this inner stage were doors through which the main stage was entered. Besides the inner and outer stages there were no fewer than four other areas where the action of the play, or parts of it, might be performed. Immediately above the inner stage, and corresponding to it in size and shape, was another room with its front exposed. This was the upper stage, and was used for upstairs scenes, or for storage when not otherwise in use. In front of this was a narrow railed gallery, which could be used for balcony scenes, or ones requiring the walls of a castle or the ramparts of a fortress. On either side of it and on the same level was a window-stage, so-called because it consisted of a small balcony enclosed by windows that opened on hinges. This permitted actors to stand inside and speak from the open windows to others on the main stage below. In all it was a very versatile multiple stage and gave the dramatist and producer much more freedom in staging than most modern theatres afford. It is interesting to note that some of the new theatres today have revived certain of the features of the Elizabethan stage.

Very little in the way of scenery and backdrops was used. The dramatist's words and the imagination of the audience supplied the lack of scenery. No special lighting effects were possible since plays were performed in the daylight that streamed in through the unroofed top of the three-tiered enclosure that was the playhouse. Usually a few standard stage-props were on hand: trestles and boards to form a table, benches and chairs, flagons, an altar, artificial trees, weapons, a man's severed head, and a few other items. Costumes were usually elaborate and gorgeous, though no attempt was made to reproduce the dress of the time and place portrayed in the play.

Play production in Shakespeare's time was clearly very different from that of ours, but we need have no doubts about the audience's response to what they saw and heard on stage. They came, they saw, and the dramatist conquered, for they kept coming back for more and more. And despite the opposition that the theatre encountered from Puritans and others, who thought it the instrument of Satan, the theatre in Shakespeare's time flourished as one of the supreme glories of a glorious age.

—DAVID G. PITT
*Memorial University of
Newfoundland.*

INTRODUCTION TO

A Midsummer Night's Dream

AN EARLY PLAY

A *Midsummer Night's Dream* was probably written in 1595-96, and therefore belongs to Shakespeare's early period as dramatist. This was his time of apprenticeship to the playwright's craft, when he was experimenting in various dramatic forms, exploring among the many materials available to him, trying out new combinations of effects, making himself familiar with the tools of his craft, and perfecting his use of them. This is not to say that A *Midsummer Night's Dream* is a crude or amateurish play. In certain respects it is imperfect: for example, some of the characters are poorly drawn and do not always come fully to life. Yet when we take into account the manner in which the young dramatist has combined so effectively such a rich variety of materials—delightful stories, superb poetry, charming songs, moonlight and magic, rustics and fairies, aristocrats and common folk, humor, satire, and some quite serious observations on love and marriage—one can only marvel at the craftsmanship that has been able to weld it all into such a balanced, controlled, and unified whole as A *Midsummer Night's Dream* is.

FOUR STORIES IN ONE

The play contains no fewer than four distinct stories, each representing a different world and providing its own kind of comedy. The Theseus-Hippolyta story gives us the world of courtly and chivalric life, of noble blood and manners, of power and authority, of heroic deeds and heroic loves. In it we have the comedy of the ceremony and ritual of love, love that is freed from the caprices of fancy and dreams, and submitted to the order and pattern of a social pageant. In the story of the "rude mechanicals"—Bottom and his friends—we have the coarser but laughable comedy of a lower stratum in society, a farcical comedy that depends for its effects on comic character, on verbal wit and physical antics, ignorance, stupidity, and occasional though unconscious illumination, all of which is delightfully incongruous in the context of the Theseus-Hippolyta story. In their play-within-the-play of Pyramus and Thisby we have the same farcical strain carried over to a parody of romantic and tragic love. In the story of the four Athenian lovers, who represent our own world of give-and-take (in love as in other things), we have a comedy of situation combined with a gentle satire on the foibles of lovers who love at first sight, who do not know their own minds and are not certain of their own hearts. And, finally, in the story of Oberon and Titania we have a kind of composite comedy that presents both the *reductio ad absurdam* of the other main love themes and situations (a travesty of marriage and a parody of love-in-idleness) and an allegory that depicts the catastrophic effects of instability in marriage.

How has Shakespeare achieved unity in this diversity? It is achieved largely by the simple device of narrative dove-tailing, of fitting the separate stories together in such a manner that none loses its identity while, at the same time, impinging upon the others so as to affect them materially both in spirit and in form. The Theseus-Hippolyta story may be called the "framing" story of the play, the story that begins and ends the action, and both encloses the other tales and forms the main bond among them. Of the others, two are related direct-ly to the Theseus-Hippolyta story and are in a sense sub-sidiary to it: the rustics are rehearsing a play to perform at the ducal wedding, at which the fairies have come from India to be present. The fairy king and queen bring with them their quarrel over the changeling boy, and it is this that causes, through the intervention of Puck at Oberon's behest, the many delightful muddles of the lovers' story. This last story comes rather by accident or coincidence into the orbits of the others and is affected by rather than affects their action. While Theseus is instrumental in enforcing the edict that sends the four lovers into the wood, it is entirely accidental, though very appropriate, that it should be the same wood near Athens in which the rustics have chosen to rehearse and the fairies to gather. Thus, the three groups of characters, each with its own private concerns, are thrown together in the wood, and this wood, where the laws of nature are sus-pended and magic rules, becomes the main locale of the en-tire action of the play, and the atmosphere of moonlight and flowers that pervades it the atmosphere that envelops the whole. Thus the fairy world of the wood and its dream vistas and its moonlight are in themselves important unifying and harmonizing elements in the play.

THE LOVE THEME

A further unifying element of the play is its primary theme: love. To say that this play has such a theme does not mean that Shakespeare has written it primarily to dramatize or illus-trate a moral or social thesis. Shakespeare never does this. Yet it is true that even in his most lighthearted comedies, and this is one of them, he is usually concerned to reflect certain ideas and attitudes that bear on human life and behavior. At the same time one should not look too closely here for a full-blown philosophy of love. Shakespeare is laughing in this play more than he is philosophizing. But are there any inferences to be drawn, say, from the quality of his laughter, or the circumstances that evoke it? Let us see.

All four stories are about love in one way or another, but that of the four Athenians is the primary love story of the play. Not only does it occupy the largest place, but it concerns people closer to ourselves than are any of the others, and is, probably for this reason, the primary context for Shakespeare's treatment of love in this play. As suggested earlier the story of the four Athenians is, at least in part, a gentle satire on the foibles of lovers who succumb to Fancy—Shakespeare's term for love that is "engendered in the eyes." His point seems to be that love which is of the eyes or of the senses alone, love-in-idleness, is a fickle and unstable love. Indeed Puck's exploits parody this fanciful love. It will be recalled that Shakespeare links the lower and the lunatic (literally, moonstruck one) in terms of how and what they *see*. Neither sees with the clear cold light of reason.

> One sees more devils than vast hell can hold,
> That is, the madman; the lover, all as frantic,
> Sees Helen's beauty in a brow of Egypt.

But is this really love? Is this the deep and lasting love that alone can make a stable marriage and a stable society? Shakespeare seems to think not. Helena observes that love "looks not with the eyes, but with the mind." And Puck exclaims at the sight of the "fond pageant" of the eye-enamored lovers, "Lord, what fools these mortals be!"

In this story, however, "the course of true love" that "never did run smooth" has been troubled by another kind of caprice than that of love-in-idleness, the irrational, passionate choice of the eyes; it is troubled also by the rational, but unfeeling, choice of a third party: Hermia's father, Egeus. His choice for Hermia has been made in a very different way from hers, but, from the viewpoint of love, it is as capricious a choice as that of love-in-idleness. Love ought not to be the subject of caprice, no matter whose. Thus the rustics' play, though a parody, shows the folly of this second kind of caprice: misguided parental authority. Love may, then, be at the mercy of blind people, and this is worse than being blind itself.

The love of Oberon and Titania is troubled too, though theirs is a married love. But Shakespeare is not here satirizing married love in a normal human relationship. Theirs is not such a relationship; after all, they are not mortals. But, most important, they have no home, no settled place of abode, no household. This is necessary to married love; for stable marriage, domesticity is the necessary complement to romance. Thus the love of Oberon and Titania is no more stable than that of Puck's victims. The Queen is as susceptible to love-in-idleness as are the mortal lovers. In contrast, Theseus and Hippolyta provide a background of sanity and stability in love for the folly and inconstancy of the others. Both have had their time of love-in-idleness, but now they represent the settled and untroubled love that, though still a passion, has been ordered and tempered by reason.

What, then, is Shakespeare's attitude toward marriage in so far as this play reflects it? Theseus early in the play sets the single over against the married state, saying that the former is "thrice-blessed" but the latter "earthlier-happy." Shakespeare does not debate the question, but he is clearly not on the side of "single blessedness." And yet he seems to say that it is better to "wither on the virgin thorn" than marry without love. This is a typical Renaissance attitude, in its insistence both on love as essential in marriage and on marriage as preferable to celibacy. For him, too, marriage should be the natural goal of love between man and woman. In this he is opposing the Mediæval notion of Courtly Love, which saw love outside of marriage as a possible end in itself.

Shakespeare also suggests that stability in marriage is necessary to ensure the stability of the ordered scheme of things—of society and even of nature itself. For the Oberon-Titania story may be read as an allegory having a meaning for human life and society. Titania may be taken to represent the moon (her name is one of several for Diana, the moon goddess) and Oberon the sun (see III, ii, 389-395). The changeling boy, then, may represent the day. Whose is the day, the moon's or the sun's? The question is not easy to answer, for a day includes both light and darkness, being the twenty-four hour span from midnight to midnight. It actually belongs to them both in partnership. But the elemental powers quarrel, and nature is turned topsy-turvy. Titania gives us a long and vivid description of nature laid waste, adding that "this same progeny of evils comes/From our debate" (III, i). The governing forces in nature must agree, must function in harmony, else all is disorder and disaster. Likewise in love and marriage, for marriage is the great stabilizer of society as the union of sun and moon is of nature.

THE CHARACTERS

As we have noted, this is an early play. It was written before Shakespeare had achieved his full powers in dramatic characterization. Hence, it is not surprising that, in *A Midsummer Night's Dream*, some of the qualities are lacking that make dramatic characters both lifelike and unique, both recognizable as human beings and yet different from anyone we have met before or are likely to meet again. Even so, the characters in this play, particularly the human ones, are never merely faceless names.

The fairies, perhaps, ought not to be judged in these terms anyway. They are a different order of beings to start with. Who are we to pass judgment on "every elf and fairy sprite"? Yet both Titania and Oberon, king and queen of Fairyland, are much like their human counterparts: dignified, regal, and courteous, yet, like them too, moved by such passions as jealousy and pride. Puck is more difficult to see as having any truly human counterpart; he is simply a quintessence of playful knavishness, good humor, gay spirits, cheerful and swift obedience. How could there be his equal amongst us monotonous mortals?

Of the mortals in the play Theseus and Hippolyta are (apart from the rustics) the most distinctly drawn and fully realized. Providing a centre of stability—in love as in temperament—in the midst of so much inconstancy and folly, they stand for intelligence, imagination, and common sense. They have passed through their time of love-in-idleness, and now have achieved the mature and settled love of people who know both their own hearts and their own minds. Here we find no quarrels over changelings, no passing infatuations, no falling in love with asses' heads. Shakespeare has not, however, pictured them as identical personalities. Theseus has undoubtedly the greater intellectual powers. Hippolyta's common-sense judgement of the rustics' play is that it is "the silliest stuff that ever I heard." But Theseus, with deeper imaginative insight, replies that "The best in this kind are but shadows; and the worst are no worse, if imagination amend them." His is the more profound judgment, for it is born of imagination as well as of intellect. The Duke and his Queen respectively represent, perhaps, imagination and common sense. If so, their marriage will be eminently successful.

The four Athenian lovers are for the most part rather vaguely drawn, although there is some differentiation among them. Lysander, for example, is more amiable than Demetrius, who is somewhat harsh and irascible though not unlikeable. The two women are rather more fully delineated and distinguished. In general, they stand in contrast to each other in both appearance and temperament. Hermia is short and dark, and has the more forceful personality of the two. She is vivacious and a bit quick tempered. We are told that "She was a vixen when she went to school; and though she be but little, she is fierce." Yet she is modest, affectionate, and loyal. We doubt that she will ever become a shrewish wife. Helena is tall and blonde, and has "no gift at all in shrewishness." She is quieter than Hermia, more easygoing, and more stable in temperament. At times she seems less able than Hermia to cope with the strange and perplexing situations into which the caprices of love and magic thrust her, appearing almost a little helpless and pathetic. Both evoke our sympathies and our affection, and this in itself speaks well for Shakespeare's burgeoning power to endow with life the "airy nothing" of his imagination. In Hermia and Helena, we can see, I think, a foreshadowing of his later memorable duo-heroines—Rosalind and Celia, Viola and Olivia, Hero and Beatrice—but he still has far to go to reach the full-blown character portrayals of his later comedies.

The rustics are, however, by far the most vivid, solid, and fully realized characters in the play. And this is so largely because Shakespeare has drawn them not from books but from life, from people he has known and observed. He has, of course, exaggerated them, made them brighter or dimmer, sadder or funnier, wiser or more foolish than they are in life, but thereby he has made them all the more substantial and real. And in a play that has so much of air and gossamer, of moonlight and flowers, it is good to have such "hempen homespuns . . . swaggering here." The gossamer is all the finer and more delicate because the home-spun is so palpable and solid. All of them are "hard-handed men . . . which never laboured in their minds till now," yet Shakespeare has succeeded in giving each some individuating characteristic. It is, nevertheless, bully Nick Bottom, the weaver, who stands out most sharply among the others. He is the most talkative, most bumptious, most conceited, and most absurd of all the clownish company, yet he is the most amiable, most poetic, and most enthusiastic and romantic of them too. He is a walking and talking paradox in the same way that Falstaff is a hyperbole. Of course, Falstaff is one of his direct lineal descendants, for in Bottom Shakespeare gave us the first of his great comic creations.

THE TITLE

It is sometimes asked why Shakespeare named this play as he did, when Duke Theseus makes clear (IV, i, 132-3) that the events in it do not take place on Midsummer Night, but rather on May Day or on the eve of May Day. The answer, I think, is that Shakespeare conceived of the strange happenings in the play, the fantastic confusions, the changing tableaux, the mixtures of the serious and the farcical, the realistic and the romantic, the natural and the supernatural, as having the quality of events in a dream, if not at times, indeed, in a nightmare. Puck at the very end of the play suggests to the audience that this, indeed, is how the play should be understood. For while Shakespeare does use the play to make certain observations on love, it is a piece of entertainment that it must finally be judged. And he is telling his audience not to judge it by the logic of ordinary experience. It must rather be seen as a fanciful romp of the imagination, such as one might encounter in the world of dream, where reason and logic are laid asleep and fancy and imagination left free to do as they will. He calls it a *midsummer* night's dream, because Midsummer Night was traditionally regarded as a time when all kinds of strange things might happen, when fairies, hobgoblins, and puckish spirits roamed abroad playing pranks on the unwary, especially lovers. Above all, it was the night when maidens dreamed of love. For a play in which the theme of love is woven into a tale of fairies and magic and such happenings as are met only in dreams, no other title could have been so apt.

—David G. Pitt
Memorial University of Newfoundland

STUDY QUESTIONS

ACT I

1. The first act of a play is usually called the *exposition*. Its function is to inform us of what we need to know in order to understand and appreciate what is to follow, to introduce some of the characters, to establish the mood and atmosphere of the play, and get the action off to a good start. Discuss the first act of this play as exposition.

2. What ideas on love and marriage are introduced quite early in this act? How important are they to the play as a whole?

3. Find references to moonlight and flowers in this act, and show how these help to create the appropriate atmosphere for the events that follow.

4. From their speeches in this act, write brief preliminary estimates of the character of each of Theseus, Egeus, Hermia, Demetrius, and Lysander.

5. Why do you think Shakespeare uses prose instead of verse in Scene ii?

6. In what different way does Shakespeare create humour in Scene ii?

7. How does Shakespeare in this scene suggest that Bottom will play a larger part in subsequent developments than the other rustics? What are your first impressions of him?

8. If you can, read the complete story of Pyramus and Thisby (in *Bulfinch's Mythology*, for example), and say why you think Shakespeare chose this particular tale for the rustics to perform.

ACT II

1. What new matter is introduced into the play at the beginning of Act II, and how does Shakespeare link it with what has gone before?
2. What devices does Shakespeare use to create an atmosphere appropriate to the fairy element in the play?
3. How does Puck's account of himself (Scene i) look forward to the part he is to play later?
4. There are some fine poetical passages in Scene i. Select three that particularly appeal to you and discuss (a) their qualities as poetry, and (b) their contribution to the dramatic action.
5. The introduction of the magic flower provides the dramatist with many possibilities for interesting and entertaining situations. How does he, in Scene i, suggest the dramatic potentialities of this element of magic, and how do these suggestions heighten dramatic tension at this point? Do you think the audience can foresee all or any of the possibilities for error and confusion inherent in Puck's mission? Explain.
6. Most of Scene ii is in rhymed verse. Does this seem appropriate here? Discuss the point.
7. Lysander says, "The will of man is by his reason sway'd." In what way is this ironic here? What other examples of irony do you find in this scene?
8. A wide variety of imagery is used in Act II. Illustrate this variety, and briefly discuss both the poetic and dramatic significance of some of the images.

ACT III

1. In the third act of a Shakespearean play usually occurs the *crisis*. This is the chief turning point in the complications of the plot, the point at which the ascending action reaches its peak and begins to move toward a resolution. Is this true of this play? If so, where precisely would you say that the turning point occurs? Give your reasons for choosing this point.
2. Do you think that Shakespeare intends to satirize actors and playwrights in Scene i? Discuss.
3. The perception of the incongruous makes us laugh. Give specific instances of incongruity that appear in the Titania-Bottom affair at the end of Scene i. Which do you think funniest? Why?
4. What further information are we given by Puck in Scene ii about the same affair? Is there any advantage in having this told us instead of shown us?
5. Write a short prose account of the events of Scene ii from

the entry of Demetrius and Hermia to the end of the scene. Does it make more plausible reading as drama or as a prose story? Why?

6. Briefly sketch the characters of the four Athenian lovers as they appear in Scene ii. Do they appear to have changed in any respects since Act I? If so, in what respects?

7. How is the happy outcome of all the errors and confusions assured by the end of Scene ii?

ACT IV

1. "The real *denouement* of this play comes in Act IV, rather than, as is customary, in Act V, which is really an epilogue." Discuss Act IV in this light. Is it an effective and satisfying *denouement*? Why? (*Denouement* means the final unraveling of the complications of the plot, the ultimate outcome of it all.)

2. How does Shakespeare in Scene i ensure that the humorous quality of the play is not overshadowed by the purely narrative concerns of winding up the story satisfactorily?

3. What purposes are served by Scene ii?

ACT V

1. Do you think that Shakespeare, having wound up the main stories of the play in Act IV, ought to have ended the play with that act? Justify your answer.

2. How is this act linked at the beginning of Scene i with the preceding act?

3. Write a paraphrase of the speech by Theseus beginning, "More strange than true . . ."

4. Write a mock-serious review of the performance of "Pyramus and Thisby."

5. Give three examples of unintentional comedy provided by Bottom and his friends in the presentation of their play.

6. Do you think that "Pyramus and Thisby" is an appropriate "play" to include in the context of *A Midsummer Night's Dream*? Why?

7. How do the songs and dances at the end contribute to the total impression created by the play? Discuss briefly.

8. Give in your own words the gist of Puck's closing speech.

General Questions

1. How does Shakespeare provide for the plausible coming together of the four groups of characters in the play?

2. Discuss *A Midsummer Night's Dream* as popular entertainment, paying particular attention to the methods and

devices used to arouse and maintain the interest of the audience.

3. *A Midsummer Night's Dream* is notable for the variety of its sources of interest. List as many of these as you can, underlining those that you consider the most effective.

4. From your knowledge of the Globe Theatre (see Introduction) describe how any three scenes in the play might have been presented there.

5. Write an essay on one or more of the following in *A Midsummer Night's Dream:* (a) humor, (b) atmosphere and mood, (c) contrast, (d) figurative language, (e) lyrical elements, (f) farce.

6. The play contains many references to the moon. Why do you think this is so? List ten such references and state briefly the significance of any four.

7. This play has been described as a comedy of incident rather than of character. Discuss it in this light.

8. Identify each of the following passages by speaker and occasion, state its meaning and its bearing, if any, on the dramatic action, and indicate what light it may shed on the character of the speaker:

   (a) Thrice-blessed they that master so their blood,
       To undergo such maiden pilgrimage,
       But earthlier happy is the rose distill'd,
       Than that which, withering on the virgin thorn,
       Grows, lives, and dies in single blessedness.

   (b) Things base and vile, holding no quantity,
       Love can transpose to form and dignity:
       Love looks not with the eyes, but with the mind;
       And therefore is wing'd Cupid painted blind:

   (c) The fairy-land buys not the child of me.
       His mother was a vot'ress of my order . . .
       But she, being mortal, of that boy did die;
       And for her sake do I rear up her boy,
       And for her sake I will not part with him.

   (d) These things seem small and undistinguishable,
       Like far-off mountains turned into clouds.

   (e) The best in this kind are but shadows; and the worst
       are no worse, if imagination amend them.

A MIDSUMMER NIGHT'S DREAM

DRAMATIS PERSONAE

THESEUS, *Duke of Athens.*

EGEUS, *father to Hermia.*

LYSANDER, } *in love with Hermia.*
DEMETRIUS,

PHILOSTRATE, *master of the revels to Theseus.*

QUINCE, *a carpenter.*

SNUG, *a joiner.*

BOTTOM, *a weaver.*

FLUTE, *a bellows-mender.*

SNOUT, *a tinker.*

STARVELING, *a tailor.*

HIPPOLYTA, *queen of the Amazons, betrothed to Theseus.*

HERMIA, *daughter to Egeus, in love with Lysander.*

HELENA, *in love with Demetrius.*

OBERON, *king of the fairies.*

TITANIA, *queen of the fairies.*

PUCK, *or Robin Goodfellow.*

PEAS-BLOSSOM,
COBWEB, } *fairies.*
MOTH,
MUSTARD-SEED,

PYRAMUS,
THISBE,
WALL, } *characters in the interlude perform'd*
MOONSHINE, *by the Clowns.*
LION,

Other FAIRIES *attending their* KING *and* QUEEN.
ATTENDANTS ON THESEUS *and* HIPPOLYTA

SCENE—*Athens, and a wood near it.*

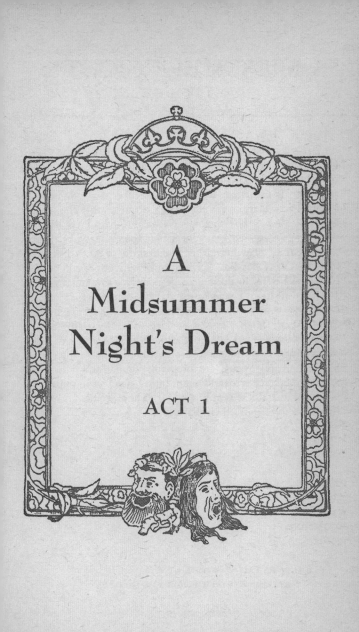

A Midsummer Night's Dream

ACT 1

ACT I

As the play opens, Theseus, Duke of Athens, is about to wed Hippolyta, Queen of the Amazons, and preparations are in progress. But the Duke is approached by Egeus, who demands, according to Athenian law, that the Duke pass judgment on his daughter Hermia for her refusal to marry his choice of a husband for her. His choice is Demetrius, who loves her, but she prefers Lysander, who loves her, too. The Duke decrees that she must obey her father or either die or go to a nunnery for the rest of her life. She has until Theseus' wedding day, four days hence, to decide. In desperation, she and Lysander agree to meet in a wood near Athens, whence they are followed by Demetrius, who has been told of the escape by Hermia's friend Helena, herself in love with Demetrius though he has already jilted her. In the meantime, a group of Athenian craftsmen, whose names are Bottom, Quince, Flute, Snug, Starveling, and Snout, are preparing to perform "the most lamentable comedy" of Pyramus and Thisby, as an entertainment for the ducal wedding night. They decide to meet in the wood to rehearse their play.

ACT I. Scene I.

Athens. The palace of THESEUS.

Enter THESEUS, HIPPOLYTA, PHILOSTRATE, *and* ATTENDANTS.

THESEUS.

Now, fair Hippolyta, our nuptial hour
Draws on apace;[1] four happy days bring in
Another moon: but, O, methinks, how slow
This old moon wanes! she lingers[2] my desires
Like to a step-dame,[3] or a dowager,
Long withering out a young man's revenue.[4]

HIPPOLYTA.

Four days will quickly steep themselves in night;
Four nights will quickly dream away the time;
And then the moon, like to a silver bow
New-bent in heaven, shall behold the night
Of our solemnities.[5]

---

[1] **Draws on apace:** rapidly approaches.
[2] **lingers:** prolongs.
[3] **step-dame** stepmother; **dowager:** widow.
[4] **Long withering out a young man's revenue:** the long drawn-out process of shrinking his inheritance.
[5] **solemnities:** the solemn rites of marriage.

THESEUS.

Go, Philostrate,

Stir up the Athenian youth to merriments;
Awake the pert[1] and nimble spirit of mirth:
Turn melancholy forth to funerals,—
The pale companion[2] is not for our pomp.

[Exit PHILOSTRATE.

Hippolyta, I woo'd thee with my sword,
And won thy love, doing thee injuries;
But I will wed thee in another key,
With pomp, with triumph,[3] and with revelling.

Enter EGEUS and his daughter HERMIA, LYSANDER, and
DEMETRIUS.

EGEUS.

Happy be Theseus, our renowned duke![4]

THESEUS.

Thanks, good Egeus: what's the news with thee?

EGEUS.

Full of vexation come I, with complaint
Against my child, my daughter Hermia.
Stand forth, Demetrius. My noble lord,
This man hath my consent to marry her.
Stand forth, Lysander: and, my gracious duke,
This hath bewitch'd the bosom of my child:—
Thou, thou, Lysander, thou hast given her rimes,
And interchanged love-tokens with my child:
Thou hast by moonlight at her window sung,
With feigning[5] voice, verses of feigning love;
And stol'n the impression of her fantasy[6]
With bracelets of thy hair, rings, gauds,[7] conceits,[8]

---

[1] **pert:** lively. [2] **pale companion:** sad fellow. [3] **triumph:** public festivity; pageantry. [4] **duke:** leader. [5] **feigning:** lying; misleading. [6] **stol'n the impression of her fantasy:** captured her imagination. [7] **gauds:** cheap trinkets; toys. [8] **conceits:** tricks.

Knacks,[1] trifles, nosegays, sweetmeats,—messengers
Of strong prevailment[2] in unharden'd [3] youth:
With cunning hast thou filch'd [4] my daughter's heart;
Turn'd her obedience, which is due to me,
To stubborn harshness:—and, my gracious duke,
Be it so she will not here before your Grace
Consent to marry with Demetrius,
I beg the ancient privilege of Athens,—
As she is mine, I may dispose of her:
Which shall be either to this gentleman
Or to her death, according to our law
Immediately[5] provided in that case.

THESEUS.

What say you, Hermia? be advised,[6] fair maid:
To you your father should be as a god;
One that composed your beauties; yea, and one
To whom you are but as a form in wax,
By him imprinted, and within his power
To leave the figure, or disfigure it.
Demetrius is a worthy gentleman.

HERMIA.

So is Lysander.

THESEUS.

　　　　　In himself he is;
But in this kind,[7] wanting your father's voice,[8]
The other must be held the worthier.

HERMIA.

I would my father lookt but with my eyes.

---

[1] **knacks**: knickknacks. [2] **prevailment**: persuasion. [3] **unharden'd**: susceptible. [4] **filch'd**: stolen. [5] **immediately**: expressly. [6] **be advised**: take heed. [7] **in this kind**: in this respect (as a husband). [8] **wanting your father's voice**: lacking your father's approval.

THESEUS.

Rather your eyes must with his judgement look.

HERMIA.

I do entreat your Grace to pardon me.
I know not by what power I am made bold,
Nor how it may concern my modesty[1],
In such a presence here to plead my thoughts;
But I beseech your Grace that I may know
The worst that may befall me in this case,
If I refuse to wed Demetrius.

THESEUS.

Either to die the death, or to abjure[2]
For ever the society of men.
Therefore, fair Hermia, question your desires;
Know of your youth,[3] examine well your blood,[4]
Whether, if you yield not to your father's choice,
You can endure the livery of a nun;[5]
For aye to be in shady cloister mew'd,[6]
To live a barren sister all your life,
Chanting faint[7] hymns to the cold fruitless moon.
Thrice-blessed they that master so their blood,
To undergo such maiden pilgrimage,[8]
But earthlier-happy is the rose distill'd [9]
Than that which, withering on the virgin thorn,
Grows, lives, and dies in single blessedness.

HERMIA.

So will I grow, so live, so die, my lord,
Ere I will yield my virgin patent[10] up
Unto his lordship, whose unwished yoke
My soul consents not to give sovereignty.

THESEUS.

Take time to pause; and, by the next new moon,—

---

[1] concern my modesty: affect my reputation. [2] abjure: give up.
[3] know of your youth: think of your youth. [4] blood: disposition;
passions. [5] livery of a nun: a nun's habit; the way of life of a nun.
[6] mew'd: enclosed; shut up. [7] faint: spiritless; without feeling.
[8] maiden pilgrimage: a new way of life. [9] distill'd: made into per-
fume. [10] virgin patent: the right to remain a virgin.

The sealing-day betwixt my love and me,
For everlasting bond of fellowship,—
Upon that day either prepare to die
For disobedience to your father's will,
Or else to wed Demetrius, as he would;
Or on Diana's altar to protest[1]
For aye[2] austerity and single life.

DEMETRIUS.

Relent, sweet Hermia:—and, Lysander, yield
Thy crazed [3] title to my certain right.

LYSANDER.

You have her father's love, Demetrius;
Let me have Hermia's: do you marry him.

EGEUS.

Scornful Lysander! true, he hath my love,—
And what is mine my love shall render him;
And she is mine,—and all my right of her
I do estate[4] unto Demetrius.

LYSANDER.

I am, my lord, as well derived [5] as he,
As well possest;[6] my love is more than his;
My fortunes every way as fairly rank'd,[7]
If not with vantage,[8] as Demetrius';
And, which is more than all these boasts can be,
I am beloved of beauteous Hermia:
Why should not, I, then, prosecute my right?
Demetrius, I'll avouch it to his head,
Made love to Nedar's daughter, Helena,
And won her soul; and she, sweet lady, dotes,
Devoutly dotes, dotes in idolatry,
Upon this spotted and inconstant man.

THESEUS.

I must confess that I have heard so much,

---

[1] **protest**: vow. [2] **For aye**: forever. [3] **crazed**: weak. [4] **estate**: bequeath.
[5] **as well derived**: of equal birth. [6] **As well possest**: as rich. [7] **fairly rank'd**: well placed. [8] **If not with vantage, as Demetrius'**: if not superior to Demetrius'.

And with Demetrius thought to have spoke thereof;
But, being over-full of self-affairs,[1]
My mind did lose it. But, Demetrius, come;
And come, Egeus; you shall go with me,
I have some private schooling[2] for you both.
For you, fair Hermia, look you arm[3] yourself
To fit your fancies to your father's will;
Or else the law of Athens yields you up—
Which by no means we may extenuate[4]—
To death, or to a vow of single life.
Come, my Hippolyta: what cheer, my love?
Demetrius, and Egeus, go along:
I must employ you in some business
Against our nuptial; and confer with you
Of something nearly that concerns[5] yourselves.

EGEUS.

With duty and desire we follow you.

[*Exeunt* THESEUS, HIPPOLYTA, EGEUS, DEMETRIUS, *and* TRAIN.

LYSANDER.

How now, my love! why is your cheek so pale?
How chance the roses there do fade so fast?

HERMIA.

Belike[6] for want of rain, which I could well
Beteem[7] them from the tempest of my eyes.

LYSANDER.

Ay me! for aught that I could ever read,
Could ever hear by tale or history,
The course of true love never did run smooth;
But, either it was different in blood,[8]—

HERMIA.

O cross! too high to be enthrall'd to low![9]

---

[1] **self-affairs**: my own business. [2] **schooling**: reprimand. [3] **arm**: prepare.
[4] **extenuate**: mitigate; weaken. [5] **nearly that concerns**: that nearly
concerns. [6] **Belike**: it is likely. [7] **Beteem**: grant. [8] **different in blood**:
disparity in status of birth. [9] **O cross! too high to be enthrall'd to
low!**: what a cross it is to bear that one of too high rank should be
enslaved by love for someone beneath her.

LYSANDER.
...n, to you: our minds we will unfold:
...orrow night, when Phœbe[1] doth behold
...silver visage in the watery glass,[2]
...king with liquid pearl the bladed grass,—
...me that lovers' flights doth still conceal,—
...ough Athens' gates have we devised[3] to steal.

HERMIA.
...d in the wood, where often you and I
...on faint primrose-beds were wont to lie,
...mptying our bosoms of their counsel sweet,
...ere my Lysander and myself shall meet;
...d thence from Athens turn away our eyes,
... seek new friends and stranger companies.
...rewell, sweet playfellow: pray thou for us;
...d good luck grant thee thy Demetrius!—
...ep word,[4] Lysander: we must starve our sight
...m lovers' food[5] till morrow deep midnight.

LYSANDER.
...ill, my Hermia.   [Exit HERMIA.
          Helena, adieu:
...you on him, Demetrius dote[6] on you!

                                        [Exit.

HELENA.
... happy some o'er other-some can be![7]
...ough Athens I am thought as fair as she.
...what of that? Demetrius thinks not so;
...vill not know what all but he do know:
...as he errs, doting on Hermia's eyes,
...admiring of his qualities.
...gs base[8] and vile, holding no quantity,[9]
...can transpose to form and dignity:
...looks not with the eyes, but with the mind;

...be: goddess of the moon. [2] watery glass: the sea. [3] devised:
...d. [4] keep word: keep your promise. [5] starve our sight/From
...food: deprive themselves of the pleasure of feasting their
...each other. [6] dote on you: love you extravagantly. [7] How
...some o'er other-some can be: how much happier some people
...others. [8] base: worthless. [9] quantity: substance.

LYSANDER.
Or else misgraffed[1] in respect of years,—

HERMIA.
O spite! too old to be engaged to young!

LYSANDER.
Or else it stood[2] upon the choice of friends,—

HERMIA.
O hell! to choose love by another's eyes!

LYSANDER.
Or, if there were a sympathy[3] in choice,
War, death, or sickness did lay siege to it,[4]
Making it momentany[5] as a sound,
Swift as a shadow, short as any dream;
Brief as the lightning in the collied[6] night,
That, in a spleen,[7] unfolds[8] both heaven and earth,
And ere a man hath power to say, 'Behold!'
The jaws of darkness do devour it up:
So quick bright things come to confusion.[9]

HERMIA.
If, then, true lovers have been ever crost,
It stands as an edict in destiny:[10]
Then let us teach our trial patience,
Because it is a customary cross,
As due to love as thoughts, and dreams, and sighs,
Wishes, and tears, poor fancy's[11] followers.

LYSANDER.
A good persuasion: therefore, hear me, Hermia.
I have a widow aunt, a dowager
Of great revenue, and she hath no child:
From Athens is her house remote seven leagues;
And she respects[12] me as her only son.
There, gentle Hermia, may I marry thee;
And to that place the sharp Athenian law

---

[1] misgraffed: misgrafted; mismated. [2] stood: depended. [3] a sympathy:
an agreement. [4] lay siege to it: put it to the test. [5] momentany:
from the Latin momentaneus; fleeting; transitory. [6] collied: darkened;
literally, smutted with coal. [7] a spleen: a fit of spiteful anger. [8] unfolds: reveals. [9] confusion: destruction. [10] an edict in destiny: fate's
decree. [11] fancy's: love's. [12] respects: regards.

Cannot pursue us. If thou lovest me, then,
Steal forth thy father's house to-morrow night;
And in the wood, a league without[1] the town,
Where I did meet thee once with Helena,
To do observance to a morn of May,
There will I stay[2] for thee.

HERMIA.

My good Lysander!
I swear to thee, by Cupid's strongest bow,
By his best arrow with the golden head,[3]
By the simplicity[4] of Venus' doves,
By that which knitteth souls and prospers loves,
And by that fire which burn'd the Carthage queen,[5]
When the false Troyan[6] under sail was seen;
By all the vows that ever men have broke,
In number more than ever women spoke;—
In that same place thou hast appointed me,
To-morrow truly will I meet with thee.

LYSANDER.

Keep promise, love. Look, here comes Helena.

Enter HELENA.

HERMIA.

God speed fair Helena! whither away?

HELENA.

Call you me fair? that fair again unsay.
Demetrius loves your fair:[7] O happy fair!
Your eyes are lode-stars;[8] and your tongue's sweet air
More tuneable[9] than lark to shepherd's ear,
When wheat is green, when hawthorn buds appear.
Sickness it catching: O, were favour[10] so,

---

[1] **without:** outside. [2] **stay:** wait. [3] **golden head:** the arrow Cupid used to inspire love was supposed to be tipped with gold. [4] **simplicity:** artlessness; innocence (the doves were sacred to Venus). [5] **Carthage queen:** Dido, who killed herslf on a funeral pyre because of her hopeless love for Aeneas. [6] **Troyan:** Trojan. [7] **fair:** beauty. [8] **Your eyes are lode-stars:** your eyes draw him to you; lodestars are the pole stars by which sailors charted their course. [9] **tuneable:** tuneful. [10] **favour:** personal appearance.

Yours would I catch, fair Hermia! ere I go,
My hair should catch your hair, my eye your e[ye,]
My tongue should catch your tongue's sweet n[...]
Were the world mine, Demetrius being bated,[1]
The rest I'ld give to be to you translated.[2]
O, teach me how you look; and with what art
You sway the motion of Demetrius' heart!

HERMIA.

I frown upon him, yet he loves me still.[3]

HELENA.

O, that your frowns would teach my smiles such skil[l]

HERMIA.

I give him curses, yet he gives me love.

HELENA.

O, that my prayers could such affection move! [4]

HERMIA.

The more I hate, the more he follows me.

HELENA.

The more I love, the more he hateth me.

HERMIA.

His folly, Helena, is no fault of mine.

HELENA.

None, but your beauty: would that fault were mi[ne]

HERMIA.

Take comfort: he no more shall see my face;
Lysander and myself will fly this place.
Before the time I did Lysander see,
Seem'd Athens as a paradise to me:
O, then, what graces in my love do dwell,
That he hath turn'd a heaven unto a hell!

---

[1] **bated:** excepted.
[2] **to be to you translated:** to be changed or tran[s...]
[3] **still:** constantly.
[4] **move:** inspire.

And therefore is wing'd Cupid painted [1] blind:
Nor hath love's mind of any judgement taste;[2]
Wings, and no eyes, figure unheedy[3] haste:
And therefore is Love said to be a child,
Because in choice he is so oft beguiled.
As waggish[4] boys in game themselves forswear,
So the boy Love is perjured every where:
For ere Demetrius lookt on Hermia's eyne,[5]
He hail'd down oaths that he was only mine;
And when this hail some heat from Hermia felt,
So he dissolved, and showers of oaths did melt.
I will go tell him of fair Hermia's flight:
Then to the wood will he to-morrow night
Pursue her; and for this intelligence[6]
If I have thanks, it is a dear expense:[7]
But herein mean I to enrich my pain,
To have his sight thither and back again.[8]   [Exit.

Scene II.

The same. A room in quince's *house.*

Enter quince *the Carpenter,* snug *the Joiner,* bottom *the
Weaver,* flute *the Bellows-mender,* snout *the Tinker, and*
starveling *the* tailor.

quince.
Is all our company here?

bottom.
You were best to call them generally, man by man, according
to the scrip.[9]

quince.
Here is the scroll of every man's name, which is thought fit,
through all Athens, to play in our interlude before the duke

---

[1] painted: pictured. [2] Nor hath love's mind of any judgement taste:
nor is love influenced by reason. [3] unheedy: unheeding. [4] waggish:
playful; mischievous. [5] eyne: eyes. [6] intelligence: information. [7] dear
expense: a costly sacrifice on my part. [8] But herein mean I to enrich my pain/To have his sight thither and back again: but I
shall be repaid for my sacrifice by having him back where I can see
him again. [9] scrip: script; written list.

and the duchess on his wedding-day at night.

BOTTOM.

First, good Peter Quince, say what the play treats on; then read the names of the actors; and so grow to a point.[1]

QUINCE.

Marry,[2] our play is *The most lamentable comedy and most cruel death of Pyramus and Thisby.*

BOTTOM.

A very good piece of work, I assure you, and a merry.—Now, good Peter Quince, call forth your actors by the scroll.— Masters, spread yourselves.

QUINCE.

Answer as I call you.—Nick Bottom the weaver.

BOTTOM.

Ready. Name what part I am for,[3] and proceed.

QUINCE.

You, Nick Bottom, are set down for Pyramus.

BOTTOM.

What is Pyramus? a lover, or a tyrant?

QUINCE.

A lover, that kills himself most gallant for love.

BOTTOM.

That will ask some tears in the true performing of it: if I do it, let the audience look to their eyes; I will move storms, I will condole[4] in some measure. To the rest: yet my chief humour is for a tryant: I could play Ercles[5] rarely, or a part to tear a cat in,[6] to make all split.

> The raging rocks
> And shivering shocks
> Shall break the locks

---

[1] **grow to a point:** come to the point. [2] **Marry:** by the Virgin Mary. [3] **Name what part I am for:** tell me my role. [4] **condole:** lament. [5] **Ercles:** Hercules. [6] **a part/to tear a cat in:** this is probably an allusion to a phrase from *Histriomasti* (1610)—"Sirrah, this is you that would rend and tear a cat upon a stage."

Of prison-gates;
And Phibbus' car[1]
Shall shine from far,
And make and mar
The foolish Fates.

This was lofty!—Now name the rest of the players.—This is
Ercles' vein, a tryant's vein;—a lover is more condoling.[2]

QUINCE.

Francis Flute the bellows-mender.[3]

FLUTE.

Here, Peter Quince.

QUINCE.

You must take Thisby on you.

FLUTE.

What is Thisby? a wandering knight?

QUINCE.

It is the lady that Pyramus must love.

FLUTE.

Nay, faith, let not me play a woman; I have a beard coming.

QUINCE.

That's all one:[4] you shall play it in a mask, and you may speak
as small as you will.[5]

BOTTOM.

An I may hide my face, let me play Thisby too: I'll speak in a
monstrous little voice;—'Thisne,[6] Thisne,'—'Ah, Pyramus, my
lover dear! thy Thisby dear, and lady dear!'

QUINCE.

No, no; you must play Pyramus:—and, Flute, you Thisby.

---

[1] **Phibbus' car:** the chariot of Phoebus, the sun god. [2] **more condoling:** a more sympathetic role. [3] **bellows-mender:** a repairer of the
bellows of organs. [4] **That's all one:** that doesn't matter. [5] **as small
as you will:** in as feminine a voice as you are able. [6] **Thisne:** Thisby;
Bottom is probably imitating a woman's high voice in saying
"Thisne."

BOTTOM.

Well, proceed.

QUINCE.

Robin Starveling the tailor.

STARVELING.

Here, Peter Quince.

QUINCE.

Robin Starveling, you must play Thisby's mother.—Tom Snout the tinker.

SNOUT.

Here, Peter Quince.

QUINCE.

You, Pyramus' father; myself, Thisby's father;—Snug the joiner, you, the lion's part:—and, I hope, here is a play fitted.[1]

SNUG.

Have you the lion's part written? pray you, if it be, give it me, for I am slow of study.

QUINCE.

You may do it extempore,[2] for it is nothing but roaring.

BOTTOM.

Let me play the lion too: I will roar, that I will do any man's heart good to hear me; I will roar, that I will make the duke say, 'Let him roar again, let him roar again.'

QUINCE.

An you should do it too terribly, you would fright the duchess and the ladies, that they would shriek; and that were enough to hang us all.

ALL.

That would hang us, every mother's son.

---

[1] fitted: properly cast.
[2] extempore: without preparation.

BOTTOM.

I grant you, friends, if you should fright the ladies out of their wits, they would have no more discretion[1] but to hang us: but I will aggravate[2] my voice so, that I will roar you as gently as any sucking dove; I will roar you an 'twere[3] any nightingale.

QUINCE.

You can play no part but Pyramus; for Pyramus is a sweet-faced man; a proper man as one shall see in a summer's day; a most lovely, gentleman-like man: therefore you must needs play Pyramus.

BOTTOM.

Well, I will undertake it. What beard were I best to play it in?

QUINCE.

Why, what you will.

BOTTOM.

I will discharge[4] it in either your straw-colour beard, your orange-tawny beard, your purple-in-grain[5] beard, or your French-crown-colour beard, your perfect yellow.

QUINCE.

Some of your French crowns have no hair at all, and then you will play barefaced.—But, masters, here are your parts: and I am to entreat you, request you, and desire you, to con[6] them by to-morrow night; and meet me in the palace-wood, a mile without the town, by moonlight: there will we rehearse, for if we meet in the city, we shall be dogg'd[7] with company, and our devices[8] known. In the mean time I will draw a bill of

---

[1] **discretion:** choice. [2] **aggravate:** lower; Bottom again uses the wrong word. [3] **an 'twere:** as if it were. [4] **discharge:** perform. [5] **purple-in-grain:** dyed a permanent purple. [6] **con:** learn them by heart. [7] **dogg'd:** pestered. [8] **device:** plans.

properties,[1] such as our play wants.[2] I pray you, fail me not.

    BOTTOM.

We will meet; and there we may rehearse most obscenely[3] and courageously.

    QUINCE.

Take pains; be perfit:[4] adieu. At the duke's oak we meet.

    BOTTOM.

Enough; hold, or cut bow-strings.[5]   [*Exeunt.*

---

[1] **properties:** stage requisites.

[2] **wants:** lacks.

[3] **obscenely:** Bottom means obscurely (secretly).

[4] **perfit:** perfect.

[5] **hold, or cut bow-strings:** that is, whatever happens, an expression from archery.

A Midsummer Night's Dream

ACT 2

ACT II

ALREADY IN the wood near Athens is a company of fairies, who have come from India for the wedding of Theseus. They include Oberon and Titania, the fairy King and Queen, Robin Goodfellow or Puck, a knavish sprite fond of playing pranks, and a large number of other fairies attendant on the King and Queen. Soon after the act opens, we learn that all is not well among the fairies. Oberon and Titania are quarreling over "a little changeling boy," an attendant of Titania's whom Oberon wants to be his page. Their quarrel has already caused severe disturbances in nature. Oberon engages Puck to help him get the boy. Puck is to fetch a magic flower whose juice, if applied to the eyes of a sleeper, will cause him to fall in love with the first living creature he beholds upon waking. This Oberon hopes to use on Titania, securing the boy when she is magically infatuated with some monster. Puck departs on his errand, leaving Oberon to overhear the conversation of Demetrius and Helena, who have now arrived in the wood, he in quest of Hermia, and Helena in pursuit of him, though he vehemently tries to rid himself of her. When Puck shortly returns with the magic flower, Oberon decides to have him use it upon Demetrius so that he will love the devoted Helena. He himself will use it on Titania, whom he soon discovers asleep. He applies the juice to her eyes and departs just as Hermia and Lysander enter and lie down to sleep. Presently Puck appears in search of the Athenian whose eyes he has been instructed to anoint. Seeing Lysander (dressed, of course, as an Athenian), Puck assumes that he is the object of his quest, and squeezes the magic liquid upon his eyelids. When he wakens shortly after, Lysander's eyes light upon Helena, who has stopped to rest in her pursuit of Demetrius, and he falls in love with her. Helena can only think that he is mocking her, and sets off at once, Lysander in pursuit and Hermia left to follow alone.

ACT II. SCENE I.

A wood near Athens.

Enter a FAIRY *at one door and* PUCK *at another.*

PUCK.

How now, spirit! whither wander you?

FAIRY.

> Over hill, over dale,
>> Thorough bush, thorough[1] brier,
> Over park, over pale,[2]
>> Thorough flood, thorough fire,
> I do wander every where,
> Swifter than the moon's sphere;
> And I serve the fairy queen,
> To dew her orbs[3] upon the green.
> The cowslips tall her pensioners[4] be:
> In their gold coats spots you see;
> Those be rubies, fairy favours,
> In those freckles live their savours:[5]

I must go seek some dewdrops here,
And hang a pearl in every cowslip's ear,
Farewell, thou lob[6] of spirits; I'll be gone:
Our queen and all her elves come here anon.

PUCK.

The king doth keep his revels here to-night:

---

[1] **thorough:** through. [2] **pale:** enclosures; fences, forbidden areas.
[3] **orbs:** fairy rings, formed by the fairies dancing in a circle. [4] **pensioners:** an allusion to Queen Elizabeth's picked band of courtiers. the handsomest and tallest young noblemen that could be found.
[5] **savours:** delights. [6] **lob:** lubber; lout.

Take heed the queen come not within his sight;
For Oberon is passing fell [1] and wrath,
Because that she, as her attendant, hath
A lovely boy, stol'n from an Indian king;
She never had so sweet a changeling: [2]
And jealous Oberon would have the child
Knight of his train, to trace [3] the forests wild;
But she perforce withholds the loved boy,
Crowns him with flowers, and makes him all her joy:
And now they never meet in grove or green,
By fountain clear or spangled starlight sheen,
But they do square [4] that all their elves, for fear,
Creep into acorn-cups, and hide them there.

    FAIRY.

Either I mistake your shape and making quite,
Or else you are that shrewd [5] and knavish sprite
Call'd Robin Goodfellow: are you not he
That frights the maidens of the villagery;
Skim milk, and sometimes labour in the quern, [6]
And bootless [7] make the breathless housewife churn;
And sometime make the drink to bear no barm: [8]
Mislead night-wanderers, laughing at their harm:
Those that Hobgoblin call you, and sweet Puck,
You do their work, and they shall have good luck:
Are not you he?

    PUCK.

             Thou speak'st aright;
I am that merry wanderer of the night,
I jest to Oberon, and make him smile,

---

[1] **passing fell:** exceedingly fierce and wrathful. [2] **changeling:** fairies stole beautiful children, leaving elves in their place. [3] **trace:** pace. [4] **square:** quarrel. [5] **shrewd:** mischievous. [6] **quern:** a hand mill for corn. [7] **bootless:** useless; to no purpose. [8] **barm:** frothy head.

When I a fat and bean-fed horse beguile,
Neighing in likeness of a filly foal:
And sometime lurk I in a gossip's bowl,[1]
In very likeness of a roasted crab,[2]
And when she drinks, against her lips I bob,
And on her wither'd dewlap pour the ale.
The wisest aunt,[3] telling the saddest tale,
Sometime for three-foot stool mistaketh me;
Then slip I from her bum,[4] down topples she,
And 'tailor'[5] cries, and falls into a cough;
And then the whole quire[6] hold their hips and loff,[7]
And waxen[8] in their mirth, and neeze,[9] and swear
A merrier hour was never wasted [10] there.—
But room, fairy! here comes Oberon.

FAIRY.

And here my mistress,—Would that he were gone!

Enter OBERON, *at one door, with his* TRAIN, *and* TITANIA, *at*
another, with hers.

OBERON.

Ill met by moonlight, proud Titania.

TITANIA.

What, jealous Oberon!—Fairies, skip hence:
I have forsworn his bed and company.

OBERON.

Tarry, rash wanton:[11] am not I thy lord?

TITANIA.

Then I must be thy lady: but I know
When thou hast stol'n away from fairy-land,
And in the shape of Corin [12] sat all day,
Playing on pipes of corn, and versing love
To amorous Phyllida. Why art thou here,
Come from the furthest steep[13] of India,

---

[1] **bowl:** hot punch. [2] **crab:** crab apple. [3] **aunt:** old woman; biddy.
[4] **bum:** rump. [5] **'tailor:** a term of opprobrium. [6] **quire:** a gathering.
[7] **loff:** laugh. [8] **waxen:** wax; increase. [9] **neeze:** sneeze. [10] **wasted:**
spent. [11] **wanton:** capricious, undisciplined woman. [12] **Corin:** Corin
and Phyllida were traditional rustic lovers. [13] **steep:** steepe.

But that, forsooth,[1] the bouncing Amazon,
Your buskin'd [2] mistress and your warrior love,
To Theseus must be wedded? and you come
To give their bed joy and prosperity.

    OBERON.

How canst thou thus, for shame, Titania,
Glance at my credit[3] with Hippolyta,
Knowing I know thy love to Theseus?
Didst thou not lead him through the glimmering night
From Perigenia, whom he ravished?
And make him with fair Aegle break his faith,
With Ariadne and Antiopa?

    TITANIA.

These are the forgeries[4] of jealousy:
And never, since the middle summer's spring,[5]
Met we on hill, in dale, forest, or mead,[6]
By paved [7] fountain or by rushy brook,
Or in the beached margent[8] of the sea,
To dance our ringlets[9] to the whistling wind,
But with thy brawls thou hast disturb'd our sport.
Therefore the winds, piping to us in vain,
As in revenge, have suck'd up from the sea
Contagious[10] fogs; which falling in the land,
Hath every pelting[11] river made so proud,
That they have overborne their continents:[12]
The ox hath therefore stretch'd his yoke in vain,
The ploughman lost[13] his sweat; and the green corn
Hath rotted ere his youth attain'd a beard:
The fold stands empty in the drowned field,
And crows are fatted with the murrion flock;[14]
The nine-men's-morris[15] is fill'd up with mud;
And the quaint mazes in the wanton green,

---

[1] **forsooth:** truly. [2] **buskin'd:** buskined; a buskin was a leather half boot. [3] **glance at my credit:** cast aspersions on my reputation. [4] **forgeries:** fabrications; lies. [5] **middle summer's spring:** the beginning of midsummer. [6] **mead:** meadow. [7] **paved:** pebbled. [8] **margent:** margin; edge. [9] **ringlets:** fairy rings. [10] **contagious:** poisonous; pestilential. [11] **pelting:** petty; paltry. [12] **continents:** the banks that restained them. [13] **lost:** wasted. [14] **murrion flock:** cattle dead from murrain. [15] **nine-men's morris:** the marked-off turf on which the men played a game in which the moves were similar to those of checkers.

For lack[1] of tread, are undistinguishable:
The human mortals want their winter cheer;
No night is now with hymn or carol blest:—
Therefore the moon, the governess of floods,
Pale in her anger, washes[2] all the air,
That rheumatic diseases do abound:
And thorough[3] this distemperature we see
The seasons alter: hoary-headed frosts
Fall in the fresh lap of the crimson rose;
And on old Hiems'[4] chin and icy crown
An odorous chaplet of sweet summer buds
Is, as in mockery, set: the spring, the summer,
The childing[5] autumn, angry winter, change
Their wonted liveries;[6] and the mazed [7] world,
By their increase,[8] now knows not which is which:
And this same progeny of evils comes
From our debate, from our dissension;
We are their parents and original.

OBERON.

Do you amend it, then; it lies in you:
Why should Titania cross her Oberon?
I do but beg a little changeling boy,
To be my henchman.[9]

TITANIA.

Set your heart at rest:
The fairy-land buys not the child of me.
His mother was a vot'ress[10] of my order:
And, in the spiced Indian air, by night,
Full often hath she gossipt by my side;
And sat with me on Neptune's yellow sands,
Marking[11] th' embarked traders on the flood;
When we have laught to see the sails conceive
And grow big-bellied with the wanton wind;

---

[1] lack: want. [2] washes: wets; moistens. [3] thorough: through. [4] Hiems':
winter. [5] childing: fruitful. [6] wonted liveries: usual dress. [7] mazed:
amazed. [8] increase produce. [9] henchman: attendant; page. [10] vot'ress:
worshiper. [11] marking: watching.

Which she, with pretty and with swimming gait
Following,—her womb then rich with my young squire,—
Would imitate, and sail upon the land,
To fetch me trifles, and return again,
As from a voyage, rich with merchandise.
But she, being mortal, of that boy did die;
And for her sake do I rear up her boy;
And for her sake I will not part with him.

    OBERON.

How long within this wood intend you stay?

    TITANIA.

Perchance till after Theseus' wedding-day.
If you will patiently dance in our round,[1]
And see our moonlight revels, go with us;
If not, shun me, and I will spare[2] your haunts.[3]

    OBERON.

Give me that boy, and I will go with thee.

    TITANIA.

Not for thy fairy kingdom.—Fairies, away!
We shall chide[4] downright, if I longer stay.

                [*Exit* TITANIA *with her* TRAIN.

    OBERON.

Well, go thy way: thou shalt not from this grove
Till I torment thee for this injury.—
My gentle Puck, come hither. Thou remember'st
Since once I sat upon a promontory,
And heard a mermaid,[5] on a dolphin's back,
Uttering such dulcet and harmonious breath,[6]
That the rude sea grew civil at her song,
And certain stars shot madly from their spheres,
To hear the sea-maid's music.

---

[1] **round**: ring.
[2] **spare**: avoid.
[3] **haunts**: company.
[4] **chide**: quarrel; scold.
[5] **mermaid**: siren.
[6] **breath**: song.

PUCK.

                    I remember.

OBERON.

That very time I saw—but thou couldst not—
Flying between the cold moon and the earth,
Cupid all arm'd: a certain aim he took
At a fair vestal throned by the west,[1]
And loosed his love-shaft smartly[2] from his bow,
As it should pierce a hundred-thousand hearts:
But I might see young Cupid's fiery shaft
Quencht in the chaste beams of the watery moon,
And the imperial vot'ress passed on,
In maiden meditation, fancy-free,
Yet markt I where the bolt of Cupid fell:
It fell upon a little western flower,
Before milk-white, now purple with love's wound,
And maidens call it love-in-idleness.[3]
Fetch me that flower; the herb I shew'd thee once:
The juice of it on sleeping eyelids laid
Will make or man or woman madly dote
Upon the next live creature that it sees.
Fetch me this herb; and be thou here again
Ere the leviathan[4] can swim a league.

PUCK.

I'll put a girdle round about the earth
In forty minutes.   [*Exit.*

OBERON.

              Having once this juice,
I'll watch Titania when she is asleep,
And drop the liquor of it in her eyes.
The next thing then she waking looks upon,—
Be it on lion, bear, or wolf, or bull,

---

[1] a fair vestal throned by the west: a virgin queen of the west; an allusion to Queen Elizabeth.
[2] smartly: vigorously.
[3] love-in-idleness: heartsease or pansy.
[4] leviathan: whale.

On meddling monkey or on busy ape,—
She shall pursue it with the soul of love:
And ere I take this charm off from her sight,
As I can take it with another herb,
I'll make her render up[1] her page to me.
But who comes here? I am invisible;
And I will overhear their conference.

Enter DEMETRIUS, HELENA *following him.*

DEMETRIUS.

I love thee not, therefore pursue me not.
Where is Lysander and fair Hermia?
The one I'll slay, the other slayeth me.
Thou told'st me they were stol'n unto this wood;
And here am I, and wood within this wood,[2]
Because I cannot meet my Hermia.
Hence, get thee gone, and follow me no more.

HELENA.

You draw me, you hard-hearted adamant;[3]
But yet you draw not iron, for my heart
Is true as steel: leave you your power to draw,
And I shall have no power to follow you.

DEMETRIUS.

Do I entice you? do I speak you fair?[4]
Or, rather, do I not in plainest truth
Tell you I do not nor I cannot love you?

HELENA.

And even for that do I love you the more.
I am your spaniel,[5] and, Demetrius,
The more you beat me, I will fawn on you:
Use me but as your spaniel, spurn me, strike me,
Neglect me, lose me; only give me leave,
Unworthy as I am, to follow you.
What worser place can I beg in your love,—

---

[1] render up: give up. [2] wood within this wood: enraged within this wood; the first "wood" comes from Woden, an Ango-Saxon deity, and is said by Verstegan in his "Restitution of Decayed Intelligence" (1605) to signify "fierce or furious." [3] adamant: magnet. [4] do I speak you fair: do I speak kindly to you. [5] spaniel: pet dog, fawning on you.

And yet a place of high respect with me,—
Than to be used as you use your dog?

DEMETRIUS.

Tempt not too much the hatred of my spirit;
For I am sick when I do look on thee.

HELENA.

And I am sick when I look not on you.

DEMETRIUS.

You do impeach your modesty[1] too much,
To leave the city, and commit yourself
Into the hands of one that loves you not;
To trust the opportunity of night,
And the ill counsel [2] of a desert place,
With the rich worth of your virginity.

HELENA.

Your virtue is my privilege:[3] for that
It is not night when I do see your face,
Therefore I think I am not in the night;
Nor doth this wood lack worlds of company,
For you in my respect[4] are all the world:
Then how can it be said I am alone,
When all the world is here to look on me?

DEMETRIUS.

I'll run from thee and hide me in the brakes,[5]
And leave thee to the mercy of wild-beasts.

HELENA.

The wildest hath not such a heart as you.
Run when you will, the story shall be changed,—
Apollo flies, and Daphne holds the chase;[6]
The dove pursues the griffin;[7] the mild hind
Makes speed to catch the tiger,—bootless[8] speed,
When cowardice pursues, and valour flies!

---

[1] **impeach your modesty**: hurt your reputation; expose yourself to scandel. [2] **ill counsel**: evil suggestions. [3] **privilege**: license. [4] **in my respect**: in my eyes. [5] **brakes**: thickets. [6] **Apollo flies, and Daphne holds the chase**: Apollo, struck by the golden-tipped arrow of Cupid, was madly in love with Daphne, but she had been struck by Cupid's lead-tipped arrow; he pursues her and she, about to be overtaken, calls on her father, the river god, to save her, and Peneus changes her into a laurel tree. [7] **griffin**: a mythological monster, half lion, half eagle. [8] **bootless**: useless.

DEMETRIUS.

I will not stay thy questions,[1] let me go:
Or, if thou follow me, do not believe
But I shall do thee mischief in the wood.

HELENA.

Ay, in the temple, in the town, the field,
You do me mischief. Fie, Demetrius!
Your wrongs do set a scandal on my sex:
We cannot fight for love, as men may do;
We should be woo'd, and were not made to woo.
I'll follow thee, and make a heaven of hell,
To die upon the hand I love so well.

[Exeunt DEMETRIUS *and* HELENA.

OBERON.

Fare thee well, nymph: ere he do leave this grove,
Thou shalt fly him, and he shall seek thy love.

Enter PUCK.

Hast thou the flower there? Welcome, wanderer.

PUCK.

Ay, there it is.

OBERON.

I pray thee, give it me.
I know a bank where the wild thyme blows,
Where oxlips[2] and the nodding violet grows;
Quite over-canopied with lush woodbine,
With sweet musk-roses, and with eglantine:[3]
There sleeps Titania sometime of[4] the night,
Lull'd in these flowers with dances and delight;
And there the snake throws her enamell'd skin,
Weed [5] wide enough to wrap a fairy in:
And with the juice of this I'll streak her eyes,
And make her full of hateful fantasies.
Take thou some of it, and seek through this grove:

---

[1] **I will not stay thy questions:** I shall not listen to you.
[2] **oxlips:** hybrid primrose, larger than cowslips.
[3] **eglantine:** sweetbrier.
[4] **sometime of:** sometimes during.
[5] **Weed:** robe.

A sweet Athenian lady is in love
With a disdainful youth: anoint his eyes;
But do it when the next thing he espies
May be the lady: thou shalt know the man
By the Athenian garments he hath on.
Effect it with some care, that he may prove
More fond on her than she upon her love:
And look thou meet me ere the first cock crow.

PUCK.

Fear not, my lord, your servant shall do so.   [*Exeunt.*

SCENE II.

Another part of the wood.

Enter TITANIA, *with her* TRAIN.

TITANIA.

Come, now a roundel [1] and a fairy song;
Then, for the third part of a minute, hence;—
Some, to kill cankers[2] in the musk-rose buds;
Some, war with rere-mice[3] for their leathern wings,
To make my small elves coats; and some, keep back
The clamorous owl, that nightly hoots and wonders
At our quaint spirits.[4] Sing me now asleep;
Then to your offices,[5] and let me rest.
                    Song.

FIRST FAIRY.

You spotted snakes with double tongue,[6]
    Thorny hedgehogs, be not seen;
Newts and blind-worms, do no wrong,
    Come not near our fairy queen.

---

[1] roundel: dance in a circle.
[2] cankers: canker worms.
[3] rere-mice: bats.
[4] quaint spirits: pleasant, delightful fairies.
[5] offices: duties.
[6] double tongue: forked tongue.

       Chorus.

  Philomel,[1] with melody
   Sing in our sweet lullaby;
Lulla, lulla, lullaby; lulla, lulla, lullaby:
    Never harm,
     Nor spell nor charm,
   Come our lovely lady nigh;
   So, good night, with lullaby.

  SECOND FAIRY.

Weaving spiders, come not here;
  Hence, you long-legg'd spinners, hence!
Beetles black, approach not near;
  Worm nor snail, do no offence.

       Chorus.

    Philomel, with melody, &c.

  FIRST FAIRY.

Hence, away! now all is well:
One aloof stand sentinel.

       [*Exeunt* FAIRIES. TITANIA *sleeps.*
     Enter OBERON.

  OBERON.

What thou see'st when thou dost wake,
     [*Squeezes the flower on* TITANIA's *eyelids.*
Do it for thy true-love take;
Love and languish for his sake:
Be it ounce,[2] or cat, or bear,
Pard,[3] or boar with bristled hair,
In thy eye that shall appear
When thou wakest, it is thy dear.
Wake when some vile thing is near.   [*Exit.*

---

[1] **Philomel:** the nightingale.
[2] **ounce:** lynx.
[3] **pard:** leopard.

Enter LYSANDER *and* HERMIA.

LYSANDER.

Fair love, you faint with wandering in the wood;
   And to speak troth,[1] I have forgot our way:
We'll rest us, Hermia, if you think it good,
   And tarry for the comfort of the day.

HERMIA.

Be it so, Lysander: find you out a bed;
For I upon this bank will rest my head.

LYSANDER.

One turf shall serve as pillow for us both;
One heart, one bed, two bosoms, and one troth.[2]

HERMIA.

Nay, good Lysander; for my sake, my dear,
Lie further off yet, do not lie so near.

LYSANDER.

O, take the sense, sweet, of my innocence! [3]
Love takes the meaning in love's conference.[4]
I mean, that my heart unto yours is knit,
So that but one heart we can make of it:
Two bosoms interchained with an oath;
So then two bosoms and a single troth.
Then by your side no bed-room me deny;
For lying so, Hermia, I do not lie.

HERMIA.

Lysander riddles very prettily:—
Now much beshrew[5] my manners and my pride,
If Hermia meant to say Lysander lied.
But, gentle friend, for love and courtesy
Lie further off; in human modesty,
Such separation as may well be said
Becomes a virtuous bachelor and a maid,

---

[1] **troth:** truthfully. [2] **troth:** pledged compact. [3] **take the sense, sweet, of my innocence:** understand the meaning of my innocence. [4] **Love takes the meaning in love's conference:** suspicion, not love, rules lovers' conversations; in other words, "Love thinketh no evil." [5] **beshrew:** a mild curse.

So far be distant; and, good night, sweet friend:
Thy love ne'er alter till thy sweet life end!

LYSANDER.

Amen, amen, to that fair prayer, say I;
And then end life when I end loyalty!
Here is my bed: sleep give thee all his rest!

HERMIA.

With half that wish the wisher's eyes be prest!

[*They sleep.*

Enter PUCK.

PUCK.

Through the forest have I gone,
But Athenian found I none,
On whose eyes I might approve[1]
This flower's force in stirring love.
Night and silence! who is here?
Weeds[2] of Athens he doth wear:
This is he my master said
Despised the Athenian maid;
And here the maiden, sleeping sound,
On the dank and dirty ground:—
Pretty soul! she durst not lie
Near this lack-love, this kill-courtesy.
Churl, upon thy eyes I throw
            [*Squeezes the flower on* LYSANDER'S *eyelids.*
All the power this charm doth owe.[3]
When thou wakest, let love forbid
Sleep his seat on thy eyelid:
So awake when I am gone;
For I must now to Oberon.   [*Exit.*

Enter DEMETRIUS *and* HELENA, *running.*

HELENA.

Stay, though thou kill me, sweet Demetrius.

---

[1] **approve:** prove.
[2] **weeds:** dress; garments.
[3] **owe:** own; possess.

DEMETRIUS.

I charge thee, hence, and do not haunt me thus.

HELENA.

O, wilt thou darkling leave me?[1] do not so.

DEMETRIUS.

Stay, on thy peril: I alone will go.   [*Exit.*

HELENA.

O, I am out of breath in this fond chase!
The more my prayer, the lesser is my grace.[2]
Happy is Hermia, wheresoe'er she lies;
For she hath blessed and attractive eyes.
How came her eyes so bright? Not with salt tears:
If so, my eyes are oftener washt than hers.
No, no, I am as ugly as a bear;
For beasts that meet me run away for fear:
Therefore no marvel though Demetrius
Do, as a monster, fly my presence thus.
What wicked and dissembling glass[3] of mine
Made me compare with Hermia's sphery eyne?[4]—
But who is here?—Lysander! on the ground!
Dead? or asleep?—I see no blood, no wound.—
Lysander, if you live, good sir, awake.

LYSANDER [*starting up*].

And run through fire I will for thy sweet sake.
Transparent[5] Helena! Nature shows art,[6]
That through thy bosom makes me see thy heart.
Where is Demetrius? O, how fit a word
Is that vile name to perish on my sword!

HELENA.

Do not say so, Lysander; say not so.
What though he love your Hermia? Lord, what though?
Yet Hermia still loves you: then be content.

---

[1] **darkling leave me:** leave me in the dark.
[2] **grace:** good fortune.
[3] **glass:** mirror.
[4] **sphery eyne:** starlike eyes.
[5] **Transparent:** radiant.
[6] **Nature shows art:** Nature shows her art.

LYSANDER.

Content with Hermia! No; I do repent
The tedious minutes I with her have spent.
Not Hermia, but Helena I love:
Who will not change a raven for a dove?
The will of man is by his reason sway'd;
And reason says you are the worthier maid.
Things growing are not ripe until their season:
So I, being young, till now ripe not[1] to reason;
And touching now the point of human skill,[2]
Reason becomes the marshal to my will,[3]
And leads me to your eyes; where I o'erlook
Love's stories, written in Love's richest book.

HELENA.

Wherefore was I to this keen mockery[4] born?
When at your hands did I deserve this scorn?
Is't not enough, is't not enough, young man,
That I did never, no, nor never can,
Deserve a sweet look from Demetrius' eye,
But you must flout[5] my insufficiency?
Good troth, you do me wrong,—good sooth, you do,—
In such disdainful manner me to woo.
But fare you well: perforce I must confess
I thought you lord of more true gentleness.[6]
O, that a lady, of one man refused,
Should of another therefore be abused!   [Exit.

LYSANDER.

She sees not Hermia.—Hermia, sleep thou there:
And never mayst thou come Lysander near!
For, as a surfeit of the sweetest things
The deepest loathing to the stomach brings;
Or, as the heresies that men do leave
Are hated most of those they did deceive;

---

[1] ripe not: not ripe. [2] touching now the point of human skill:
reaching the highest point of my greatness. [3] Reason becomes the
marshal to my will: reason now becomes the dictator of my actions.
[4] keen mockery: cruel joke. [5] flout: mock. [6] lord of more true
gentleness: that is, a gentleman.

So thou, my surfeit and my heresy,
Of all be hated, but the most of me!
And, all my powers, address your love and might
To honour Helen, and to be her knight!   [*Exit.*
    HERMIA [*awaking*].
Help me, Lysander, help me! do thy best
To pluck this crawling serpent from my breast!
Ay me, for pity!—what a dream was here!
Lysander, look how I do quake with fear:
Methought a serpent eat[1] my heart away,
And you sat smiling at his cruel [2] prey.—
Lysander!—what, removed?[3]—Lysander! lord!—
What, out of hearing? gone? no sound, no word?
Alack, where are you? speak, an if you hear;
Speak, of all loves! [4] I swoon almost[5] with fear.
No?—then I well perceive you are not nigh:
Either death or you I'll find immediately.   [*Exit.*

---

[1] **eat:** ate.
[2] **cruel:** helpless.
[3] **removed:** gone away.
[4] **of all loves:** for love's sake.
[5] **I swoon almost:** I almost swoon.

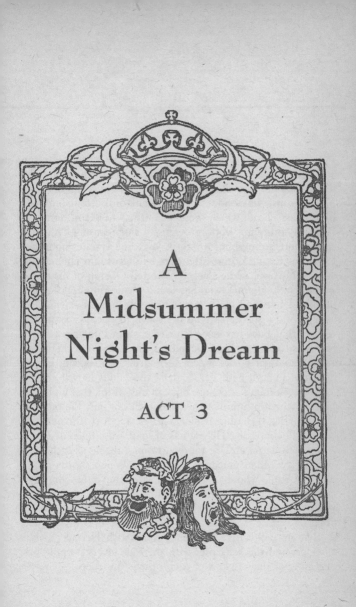

A Midsummer Night's Dream

ACT 3

ACT III

Puck, in the meantime, has come upon the rustics—Bottom and his friends—as they rehearse their play in the wood near where Titania lies sleeping with the love-juice in her eyes. Mischievously he decides to play a prank on Bottom, and gives him an ass's head, which causes the others to flee in terror. To keep his spirits up, Bottom begins to sing, causing Titania to waken and, seeing him, to fall in love. She lavishes upon him loving words and doting attention, and gives him fairy attendants of his own, while Puck goes to tell Oberon of his prank. As they talk, Hermia, who has found Demetrius, appears with him, still rejecting his love and accusing him of slaying Lysander. When she departs he lies down to sleep. Oberon now realizes that Puck has made a mistake, and while he sends him to fetch Helena anoints Demetrius himself. The others soon arrive and their voices waken Demetrius, who seeing Helena first falls in love with her. Helena thus finds herself the object of both men's affection, but can only think that a plot has been hatched to humiliate her, to which not only the men but her old friend Hermia is also a party. Hermia, for her part, can only believe that Helena has in some way stolen her lover. A double quarrel ensues, the two women raging at each other and the two men preparing for a duel. When shortly all depart, Oberon, who has been observing the imbroglio, commands Puck to darken the night so that the men will be separated and fall asleep, exhausted, before any further harm is done. He must then contrive to anoint the eyes of Lysander so that he will fall in love once more with Hermia. This is all done, and the act closes with the four lovers sleeping near one another unconscious of each other's presence.

ACT III. SCENE I.

The wood. TITANIA *lying asleep.*

Enter QUINCE, SNUG, BOTTOM, FLUTE, SNOUT, *and* STARVELING.

BOTTOM.
Are we all met?

QUINCE.
Pat,[1] pat; and here's a marvellous convenient place for our rehearsal. This green plot shall be our stage, this hawthorn-brake our tiring-house;[2] and we will do it in action as we will do it before the duke.

BOTTOM.
Peter Quince,—

QUINCE.
What say'st thou, bully Bottom?

---

[1] **Pat:** exactly.
[2] **tiring-house:** dressing room.

BOTTOM.

There are things in this comedy of *Pyramus and Thisby* that
will never please. First, Pyramus must draw a sword to kill
himself; which the ladies cannot abide. How answer you that?

SNOUT.

By'r lakin,[1] a parlous[2] fear.

STARVELING.

I believe we must leave the killing out, when all is done.

BOTTOM.

Not a whit: I have a device[3] to make all well. Write me a
prologue; and let the prologue seem to say, we will do no
harm with our swords, and that Pyramus is not kill'd indeed;
and, for the more better assurance, tell them that I Pyramus
am not Pyramus, but Bottom the weaver: this will put them
out of fear.

QUINCE.

Well, we will have such a prologue; and it shall be written in
eight and six.[4]

BOTTOM.

No, make it two more: let it be written in eight and eight.

SNOUT.

Will not the ladies be afeard of the lion?

STARVELING.

I fear it, I promise you.

BOTTOM.

Masters, you ought to consider with yourselves: to bring in,—
God shield us!—a lion among ladies is a most dreadful thing;

---

[1] **By'r lakin:** by our Ladykin (Little Lady—the Virgin Mary).

[2] **parlous:** perilous.

[3] **device:** plan.

[4] **eight and six:** that is, in alternate verses of eight and six syl-
lables.

for there is not a more fearful wild-fowl than your lion living; and we ought to look to't.

SNOUT.

Therefore another prologue must tell he is not a lion.

BOTTOM.

Nay, you must name his name, and half his face must be seen through the lion's neck; and he himself must speak through, saying thus, or to the same defect,[1]—'Ladies,'—or, 'Fair ladies, —I would wish you,'—or, 'I would request you,'—or, 'I would entreat you,—not to fear, not to tremble: my life for yours. If you think I come hither as a lion, it were pity of my life:[2] no, I am no such thing; I am a man as other men are:'— and there, indeed, let him name his name, and tell them plainly he is Snug the joiner.

QUINCE.

Well, it shall be so. But there is two hard things,—that is, to bring the moonlight into a chamber; for, you know, Pyramus and Thisby meet by moonlight.

SNUG.

Doth the moon shine that night we play our play?

BOTTOM.

A calendar, a calendar! look in the almanac; find out moon-shine, find out moonshine.

QUINCE.

Yes, it doth shine that night.

BOTTOM.

Why, then may you leave a casement of the great chamber-window, where we play, open, and the moon may shine in at

---

[1] defect: effect.
[2] it were pity of my/life: it was in fear of my life.

the casement.

QUINCE.

Ay; or else one must come in with a bush of thorns[1] and a lantern, and say he comes to disfigure,[2] or to present,[3] the person of moonshine. Then, there is another thing: we must have a wall in the great chamber; for Pyramus and Thisby, says the story, did talk through the chink of a wall.

SNUG.

You can never bring in a wall.—What say you, Bottom?

BOTTOM.

Some man or other must present wall: and let him have some plaster, or some loam, or some rough-cast[4] about him, to signify wall; and let him hold his fingers thus, and through that cranny shall Pyramus and Thisby whisper.

QUINCE.

If that may be, then all is well. Come, sit down, every mother's son, and rehearse your parts. Pyramus, you begin: when you have spoken your speech, enter into that brake;— and so every one according to his cue.

Enter PUCK *behind.*

PUCK.

What hempen home-spuns have we swaggering here, So near the cradle of the fairy queen? What, a play toward! [5] I'll be an auditor; An actor too perhaps, if I see cause.

QUINCE.

Speak, Pyramus.—Thisby, stand forth.

BOTTOM.

Thisby, the flowers of odious savours sweet,—

---

[1] **bush of thorns:** Rolfe says an old superstition identified the man in the moon with the man that gathered sticks on the Sabbath, numbers XV. 32. [2] **disfigure:** portray. [3] **present:** represent. [4] **rough-cast:** a crude lime plastering mixed with pebbles. [5] **a play toward:** a play in preparation.

QUINCE.

Odours, odours.

BOTTOM.

———odours savours sweet:
So hath thy breath, my dearest Thisby dear.—
But hark, a voice! stay thou but here awhile,
And by and by I will to thee appear.   [*Exit.*
PUCK [*Aside*].

A stranger Pyramus than e'er play'd here.   [*Exit.*

FLUTE.

Must I speak now?

QUINCE.

Ay, marry, must you; for you must understand he goes but to
see a noise that he heard, and is to come again.

FLUTE.

Most radiant Pyramus, most lily-white of hue,
Of colour like the red rose on triumphant[1] brier,
Most brisky[2] juvenal,[3] and eke[4] most lovely Jew,
As true[5] as truest horse, that yet would never tire,
I'll meet thee, Pyramus, at Ninny's tomb.

QUINCE.

'Ninus'[6] tomb,' man:—why, you must not speak that yet;
that you answer to Pyramus: you speak all your part at once,
cues and all.—Pyramus enter: your cue is past; it is, 'never
tire.'

FLUTE.

O,—As true as truest horse, that yet would never tire.

Enter PUCK, *and* BOTTOM *with an ass-head.*

BOTTOM.

If I were fair, Thisby, I were only thine:—

---

[1] **triumphant:** conquering. [2] **brisky:** brisk. [3] **juvenal:** youth. [4] **eke:**
also. [5] **true:** sound. [6] **Ninus:** in Greek mythology, the founder of the
city of Nineveh; he conquered the whole of Western Asia and
founded the first empire.

QUINCE.

O monstrous! O strange! we are haunted.—
Pray, masters! fly, masters!—Help!

[*Exit with* SNUG, FLUTE, SNOUT, *and* STARVELING.

PUCK.

I'll follow you, I'll lead you about a round,
    Through bog, through bush, through brake, through brier:
Sometime a horse I'll be, sometime a hound,
    A hog, a headless bear, sometime a fire,[1]
And neigh, and bark, and grunt, and roar, and burn,
Like horse, hound, hog, bear, fire, at every turn.   [*Exit.*

BOTTOM.

Why do they run away? this is a knavery of them to make
me afeard.

Enter SNOUT.

SNOUT.

O Bottom, thou art changed! what do I see on thee?

BOTTOM.

What do you see? you see an ass-head of your own, do you?

[*Exit* SNOUT.

Enter QUINCE.

QUINCE.

Bless thee, Bottom! bless thee! thou art translated.[2]   [*Exit.*

BOTTOM.

I see their knavery: this is to make an ass of me; to fright me,
if they could. But I will not stir from this place, do what they
can: I will walk up and down here, and I will sing, that they

---

[1] **fire**: will-o'-the-wisp.
[2] **translated**: transformed.

shall hear I am not afraid.   [*Sings.*

> The ousel-cock[1] so black of hue,
>   With orange-tawny bill,
> The throstle[2] with his note so true,
>   The wren with little quill:[3]—

TITANIA [*awaking*].

What angel wakes me from my flowery bed?

BOTTOM [*sings*].

> The finch, the sparrow, and the lark,
>   The plain-song[4] cuckoo gray,
> Whose note full many a man doth mark,
>   And dares not answer nay:—

for, indeed, who would set his wit[5] to so foolish a bird? who
would give a bird the lie, though he cry 'cuckoo' never so?[6]

TITANIA.

I pray thee, gentle mortal, sing again:
Mine ear is much enamour'd of thy note;
So is mine eye enthralled to thy shape;
And thy fair virtue's force perforce doth move me,
On the first view, to say, to swear, I love thee.

BOTTOM.

Methinks, mistress, you should have little reason for that: and
yet, to say the truth, reason and love keep little company[7] together now-a-days:—the more the pity that some honest neighbours will not make them friends. Nay, I can gleek[8] upon
occasion.

TITANIA.

Thou art as wise as thou art beautiful.

---

[1] **ousel-cock:** blackbird. [2] **throstle:** thrush. [3] **quill:** musical pipe.
[4] **plain-song:** song without variations. [5] **set his wit:** oppose his wit.
[6] **never so:** ever so much. [7] **keep little company:** have little in common. [8] **gleek:** scoff; jest.

BOTTOM.

Not so, neither: but if I had wit enough to get out of this
wood, I have enough to serve mine own turn.

TITANIA.

Out of this wood do not desire to go:
Thou shalt remain here, whether thou wilt or no.
I am a spirit of no common rate,[1]—
The summer still doth tend upon my state;[2]
And I do love thee: therefore, go with me;
I'll give thee fairies to attend on thee;
And they shall fetch thee jewels from the deep,
And sing, while thou on pressed flowers dost sleep:
And I will purge thy mortal grossness[3] so,
That thou shalt like an airy spirit go.—
Peas-blossom! Cobweb! Moth! and Mustard-seed!

Enter four FAIRIES.

FIRST FAIRY.

Ready.

SECOND FAIRY.

And I.

THIRD FAIRY.

And I.

FOURTH FAIRY.

And I.

ALL.

Where shall we go?

TITANIA.

Be kind and courteous to this gentleman,—
Hop in his walks, and gambol in his eyes;
Feed him with apricocks[4] and dewberries,

---

[1] rate: rank.
[2] **The summer still doth tend upon my estate:** the summer always
enriches my estate.
[3] **I will purge thy mortal grossness:** I will purify your human weak-
nesses.
[4] apricocks: apricots.

With purple grapes, green figs, and mulberries;
The money-bags steal from the humble-bees,[1]
And for night-tapers crop their waxen thighs,
And light them at the fiery glow-worm's eyes,
To have my love to bed and to arise;
And pluck the wings from painted butterflies
To fan the moonbeams from his sleeping eyes:
Nod to him, elves, and do him courtesies.

FIRST FAIRY.

Hail, mortal!

SECOND FAIRY.

Hail!

THIRD FAIRY.

Hail!

FOURTH FAIRY.

Hail!

BOTTOM.

I cry your worship's mercy heartily.[2]—I beseech your worship's name.

COBWEB.

Cobweb.

BOTTOM.

I shall desire you of more acquaintance, good Master Cobweb: if I cut my finger,[3] I shall make bold with you.—Your name, honest gentleman?

PEAS-BLOSSOM.

Peas-blossom.

BOTTOM.

I pray you, commend me to Mistress Squash, your mother, and to Master Peascod, your father. Good Master Peas-blossom, I shall desire you of more acquaintance too.—Your name, I beseech you, sir?

---

[1] humble-bees: bumblebees.
[2] I cry your worship's mercy heartily: I humbly beg your pardon.
[3] cut my finger, etc.: cobwebs were considered to have healing properties, and were therefore used to stop bleeding.

MUSTARD-SEED.

Mustard-seed.

BOTTOM.

Good Master Mustard-seed, I know your patience well: that
same cowardly, giant-like ox-beef hath devour'd many a
gentleman of your house: I promise you[1] your kindred hath
made my eyes water ere now. I desire you more acquaintance,
good Master Mustard-seed.

TITANIA.

Come, wait upon him; lead him to my bower.
    The moon methinks looks with a watery eye;
And when she weeps, weeps every little flower,
    Lamenting some enforced [2] chastity.
    Tie up my love's tongue, bring him silently.   [*Exeunt.*

SCENE II.

Another part of the wood.

Enter OBERON.

OBERON.

I wonder if Titania be awaked;
Then, what it was that next came in her eye,
Which she must dote on in extremity.[3]—
Here comes my messenger.
                              Enter PUCK.
                                 How now, mad spirit!
What night-rule[4] how about this haunted grove?

PUCK.

My mistress with a monster is in love.
Near to her close[5] and consecrated bower,
While she was in her dull and sleeping hour,
A crew of patches,[6] rude mechanicals,[7]

---

[1] **I promise you:** I assure you. [2] **enforced:** violated. [3] **in extremity:**
excessively. [4] **rule:** conduct. [5] **close:** hidden. [6] **patches:** fools; clowns.
[7] **rude mechanicals:** rough or untrained mechanics.

That work for bread upon Athenian stalls,
Were met together to rehearse a play,
Intended for great Theseus' nuptial day.
The shallowest thickskin[1] of that barren sort,[2]
Who Pyramus presented in their sport,
Forsook his scene, and enter'd in a brake:
When I did him at this advantage take,
An ass's nowl [3] I fixed on his head:
Anon his Thisbe must be answered,
And forth my mimic comes. When they him spy,
As wild geese that the creeping fowler eye,
Or russet-pated choughs,[4] many in sort,[5]
Rising and cawing at the gun's report,
Sever[6] themselves, and madly sweep the sky,
So, at his sight, away his fellows fly;
And, at our stamp,[7] here o'er and o'er one falls;
He murder cries, and help from Athens calls.
Their sense thus weak, lost with their fears thus strong,
Made senseless things begin to do them wrong;
For briers and thorns at their apparel snatch;
Some, sleeves,—some, hats;—from yields all things catch.
I led them on in this distracted fear,
And left sweet Pyramus translated [8] there:
When in that moment,—so it came to pass,—
Titania waked, and straightway loved an ass.

OBERON.

This falls out[9] better than I could devise.
But hast thou yet latcht[10] the Athenian's eyes
With the love-juice, as I did bid thee do?

PUCK.

I took him sleeping,—that is finisht too,—

---

[1] **thickskin**: a term of contempt for a country clown. [2] **barren sort:** dull company. [3] **nowl**: head. [4] **choughs**: jackdaws. [5] **in sort**: of a kind. [6] **sever**: separate. [7] **stamp**: stamping. [8] **translated**: transformed. [9] **falls out**: works out. [10] **lacht**: infected; caught.

And the Athenian woman by his side;
That, when he waked, of force[1] she must be eyed.

Enter HERMIA *and* DEMETRIUS.

OBERON.

Stand close: this is the same Athenian.

PUCK.

This is the woman, but not this the man.

DEMETRIUS.

O, why rebuke you him that loves you so?
Lay breath[2] so bitter on your bitter foe.

HERMIA.

Now I but chide; but I should use thee worse,
For thou, I fear, hast given me cause to curse.
If thou hast slain Lysander in his sleep,
Being o'er shoes[3] in blood, plunge in the deep,
And kill me too.
The sun was not so true unto the day
As he to me: would he have stol'n away
From sleeping Hermia? I'll believe as soon
This whole earth may be bored; and that the moon
May through the centre creep, and so displease
Her brother's[4] noontide with th' Antipodes.
It cannot be but thou hast murder'd him;
So should a murderer look,—so dead,[5] so grim.

DEMETRIUS.

So should the murder'd look; and so should I,
Pierced through the heart with your stern cruelty.
Yet you, the murderer, look as bright, as clear,
As yonder Venus in her glimmering sphere.

HERMIA.

What's this to my Lysander? where is he?
Ah, good Demetrius, wilt thou give him me?[6]

---

[1] **in force:** of necessity. [2] **breath:** words. [3] **o'er shoes:** knee deep.
[4] **brother's:** Phoebus: in mythology, the sun and moon were considered brother and sister. [5] **dead:** deadly. [6] **give him me:** give him to me.

DEMETRIUS.

I had rather give his carcass to my hounds.

HERMIA.

Out, dog! out, cur! thou drivest me past the bounds
Of maiden's patience. Hast thou slain him, then?
Henceforth be never number'd among men!
O, once tell true, tell true, even for my sake!
Durst thou have lookt upon him being awake,
And hast thou kill'd him sleeping? O brave touch!
Could not a worm,[1] an adder, do so much?
An adder did it; for with doubler tongue[2]
Than thine, thou serpent, never adder stung.

DEMETRIUS.

You spend your passion on a misprised mood:[3]
I am not guilty of Lysander's blood;
Nor is he dead, for aught that I can tell.

HERMIA.

I pray thee, tell me, then, that he is well.

DEMETRIUS.

An if I could, what should I get therefore?

HERMIA.

A privilege, never to see me more:—
And from thy hated presence part I so:
See me no more, whether he be dead or no.   [*Exit.*

DEMETRIUS.

There is no following her in this fierce vein:[4]
Here therefore for a while I will remain.
So sorrow's heaviness[5] doth heavier grow
For debt that bankrout[6] sleep doth sorrow owe;
Which now in some slight measure it will pay,

---

[1] **worm:** serpent.
[2] **doubler tongue:** more forked tongue.
[3] **misprised mood:** mistaken fancy.
[4] **vein:** mood.
[5] **heaviness:** sadness.
[6] **bankrout:** bankrupt.

If for his tender here I make some stay.[1]

                             [Lies down and sleeps.

OBERON.

What hast thou done? thou hast mistaken quite,
And laid the love-juice on some true-love's sight:
Of thy misprision[2] must perforce ensue
Some true-love turn'd, and not a false turn'd true.

PUCK.

Then fate o'er-rules; that, one man holding troth,[3]
A million fail, confounding[4] oath on oath.

OBERON.

About the wood go swifter than the wind,
And Helena of Athens look thou find:
All fancy-sick[5] she is, and pale of cheer[6]
With sighs of love, that costs the fresh blood dear:[7]
By some illusion see thou bring her here:
I'll charm his eyes against she do appear.[8]

PUCK.

I go, I go; look how I go,—
Swifter than arrow from the Tartar's bow.   *[Exit.*

OBERON.

        Flower of this purple dye,
        Hit with Cupid's archery,
          [Squeezes the flower on DEMETRIUS's *eyelids.*
        Sink in apple of his eye!
        When his love he doth espy,
        Let her shine as gloriously
        As the Venus of the sky.—
        When thou wakest, if she be by,
        Beg of her for remedy.

---

[1] **If for his tender here I make some stay:** if I wait here a while for it to offer itself. [2] **misprision:** mistake. [3] **holding troth:** keeping faith. [4] **confounding:** breaking; destroying. [5] **fancy-sick:** lovesick. [6] **cheer:** countenance. [7] **With sighs of love, that cost the fresh blood dear:** it was an old belief that every sigh caused the loss of a drop of blood. [8] **against she do appear:** in preparation for her appearance.

Enter PUCK.

PUCK.

> Captain of our fairy band,
> Helena is here at hand;
> And the youth, mistook by me,
> Pleading for a lover's fee.[1]
> Shall we their fond pageant[2] see?
> Lord, what fools these mortals be!

OBERON.

> Stand aside: the noise they make
> Will cause Demetrius to awake.

PUCK.

> Then will two at once woo one,—
> That must needs[3] be sport alone;
> And those things do best please me
> That befall preposterously.[4]

Enter HELENA *and* LYSANDER.

LYSANDER.

Why should you think that I should woo in scorn?
  Scorn and derision never come in tears:
Look, when I vow, I weep; and vows so born,
  In their nativity all truth appears.
How can these things in me seem scorn to you,
Bearing the badge of faith, to prove them true?

HELENA.

You do advance[5] your cunning more and more.
  When truth kills truth, O devilish-holy fray!
These vows are Hermia's: will you give her o'er?
  Weigh oath with oath, and you will nothing weigh:
Your vows to her and me, put in two scales,
Will even weigh; and both as light as tales.

---

[1] **a lover's fee:** a lover's reward.
[2] **fond pageant:** silly show or exhibition.
[3] **needs:** of necessity.
[4] **preposterously:** perversely.
[5] **advance:** show.

LYSANDER.

I had no judgement when to her I swore.

HELENA.

Nor none, in my mind, now you give her o'er.

LYSANDER.

Demetrius loves her, and he loves not you.

DEMETRIUS [*awaking*].

O Helen, goddess, nymph, perfect, divine!
To what, my love, shall I compare thine eyne?
Crystal is muddy. O, how ripe in show
Thy lips, those kissing cherries,[1] tempting grow!
That pure congealed white, high Taurus'[2] snow,
Fann'd with the eastern wind, turns to a crow[3]
When thou hold'st up thy hand: O, let me kiss
This princess of pure white, this seal of bliss!

HELENA.

O spite! O hell! I see you all are bent
To set against me for your merriment:
If you were civil and knew courtesy,
You would not do me thus much injury.
Can you not hate me, as I know you do,
But you must join in souls[4] to mock me too?
If you were men, as men you are in show,[5]
You would not use a gentle lady so;
To vow, and swear, and superpraise my parts,
When I am sure you hate me with your hearts.
You both are rivals, and love Hermia;
And now both rivals, to mock Helena:
A trim[6] exploit, a manly enterprise,
To conjure tears up in a poor maid's eyes
With your derision! none of noble sort[7]
Would so offend a virgin, and extort[8]
A pour soul's patience, all to make you sport.

---

[1] **cherries:** cherry lips. [2] **Taurus:** a mountain range in Asia Minor.
[3] **turns to a crow:** appears to be black (beside the whiteness of your hand). [4] **join in souls:** join with all your might. [5] **show:** appearance.
[6] **trim:** fine; nice (used ironically). [7] **of noble sort:** of a noble nature.
[8] **extort:** take away.

LYSANDER.

You are unkind, Demetrius; be not so;
For you love Hermia;—this you know I know:
And here, with all good will, with all my heart,
In Hermia's love I yield you up my part;
And yours of Helena to me bequeath,
Whom I do love, and will do to my death.

HELENA.

Never did mockers waste more idle breath.

DEMETRIUS.

Lysander, keep thy Hermia; I will none:[1]
If e'er I loved her, all that love is gone.
My heart to her but as guest-wise sojourn'd,
And now to Helen is it home return'd,
There to remain.

LYSANDER.

Helen, it is not so.

DEMETRIUS.

Disparage not the faith thou dost not know,
Lest, to thy peril, thou aby it dear.[2]—
Look, where thy love comes; yonder is thy dear.

Enter HERMIA.

HERMIA.

Dark night, that from the eye his[3] function takes,
The ear more quick of apprehension makes;
Wherein it doth impair the seeing sense,
It pays the hearing double recompense.—
Thou art not by mine eye, Lysander, found;
Mine ear, I thank it, brought me to thy sound.
But why unkindly didst thou leave me so?

LYSANDER.

Why should he stay, whom love doth press to go?

---

[1] **I will none:** that is, I will have nothing to do with her.
[2] **thou aby it dear:** it will cost you dearly.
[3] **his:** its.

HERMIA.

What love could press Lysander from my side?

LYSANDER.

Lysander's love, that would not let him bide,—
Fair Helena; who more engilds the night
Than all yon fiery O's[1] and eyes of light.
Why seek'st thou me? could not this make thee know,
The hate I bear thee made me leave thee so?

HERMIA.

You speak not as you think: it cannot be.

HELENA.

Lo, she is one of this confederacy!
Now I perceive they have conjoin'd all three
To fashion this false sport in spite of me.
Injurious[2] Hermia! most ungrateful maid!
Have you conspired, have you with these contrived
To bait[3] me with this foul derision?
Is all the counsel [4] that we two have shared,
The sisters' vows, the hours that we have spent,
When we have chid the hasty-footed time
For parting us,—O, and is all forgot?
All school-days' friendship, childhood innocence?
We, Hermia, like two artificial gods,[5]
Have with our neelds[6] created both one flower,
Both on one sampler, sitting on one cushion,
Both warbling of one song, both in one key;
As if our hands, our sides, voices, and minds,
Had been incorporate.[7] So we grew together,
Like to a double cherry, seeming parted,
But yet an union in partition;
Two lovely berries moulded on one stem;
So, with two seeming bodies, but one heart;

---

[1] O's: oes; orbs. [2] Injurious: insulting. [3] bait: torment. [4] counsel: confiidences. [5] artificial gods: creators in art. [6] neelds: needles. [7] incorporate: one person.

Two of the first, like coats in heraldry,
Due[1] but to one, and crowned with one crest.
And will you rent our ancient love asunder,
To join with men in scorning your poor friend?
It is not friendly, 'tis not maidenly:
Our sex, as well as I, may chide you for it,
Though I alone do feel the injury.

HERMIA.

I am amazed at your passionate words.
I scorn you not: it seems that you scorn me.

HELENA.

Have you not set Lysander, as in scorn,
To follow me, and praise my eyes and face?
And made your other love, Demetrius—
Who even but now did spurn me with his foot—
To call me goddess, nymph, divine, and rare,
Precious, celestial? Wherefore speaks he this
To her he hates? And wherefore doth Lysander
Deny your love, so rich within his soul,
And tender me, forsooth, affection,
But by your setting on, by your consent?
What though I be not so in grace[2] as you,
So hung upon with love, so fortunate;
But miserable most, to love unloved?
This you should pity rather than despise.

HERMIA.

I understand not what you mean by this.

HELENA.

Ay, do, persever,[3] counterfeit[4] sad looks;
Make mouths[5] upon me when I turn my back;
Wink each at other;[6] hold the sweet jest up:
This sport, well carried,[7] shall be chronicled.
If you have any pity, grace, or manners,

---

[1] due: belonging. [2] in grace: in favor. [3] persever: persevere. [4] counterfeit: feign. [5] Make mouths: make faces. [6] Wink each at other: wink at each other. [7] well carried: well managed.

You would not make me such an argument.[1]
But, fare ye well: 'tis partly mine own fault;
Which death or absence soon shall remedy.

LYSANDER.

Stay, gentle Helena; hear my excuse:
My love, my life, my soul, fair Helena!

HELENA.

O excellent!

HERMIA.

Sweet, do not scorn her so.

DEMETRIUS.

If she cannot entreat, I can compel.

LYSANDER.

Thou canst compel no more than she entreat:
Thy threats have no more strength than her prayers.—
Helen, I love thee; by my life, I do:
I swear by that which I will lose for thee,
To prove him false that says I love thee not.

DEMETRIUS.

I say I love thee more than he can do.

LYSANDER.

If thou say so, withdraw, and prove it too.

DEMETRIUS.

Quick, come!

HERMIA.

Lysander, whereto tends all this?

LYSANDER.

Away, you Ethiop![2]

DEMETRIUS.

No, no, sir;
Seem to break loose, take on as you would follow.[3]
But yet come not: you are a tame[4] man, go!

---

[1] such an argument: the butt of a joke.
[2] Ethiope: an allusion to Hermia's dark skin.
[3] take on as you would follow: pretend that you will go along with me.
[4] tame: timid; cowardly.

LYSANDER.

Hang off,[1] thou cat, thou burr! vile thing, let loose,
Or I will shake thee from me like a serpent!

HERMIA.

Why are you grown so rude? what change is this, Sweet love?

LYSANDER.

Thy love! out, tawny Tartar, out!
Out, loathed medicine! O hated potion,[2] hence!

HERMIA.

Do you not jest?

HELENA.

Yes, sooth; and so do you.

LYSANDER.

Demetrius, I will keep my word with thee.

DEMETRIUS.

I would I had your bond, for I perceive
A weak bond holds you: I'll not trust your word.

LYSANDER.

What, should I hurt her, strike her, kill her dead?
Although I hate her, I'll not harm her so.

HERMIA.

What, can you do me greater harm than hate?
Hate me! wherefore? O me! what news, my love?
Am not I Hermia? are not you Lysander?
I am as fair now as I was erewhile.[3]
Since night you loved me; yet since night you left me:
Why, then you left me,—O, the gods forbid!—
In earnest, shall I say?

LYSANDER.

Ay, by my life;

---

[1] **Hang off:** get away from me.
[2] **potion:** prison.
[3] **erewhile:** a short while ago.

And never did desire to see thee more.
Therefore be out of hope, of question, doubt;
Be certain, nothing truer; 'tis no jest
That I do hate thee, and love Helena.

HERMIA.

O me!—you juggler! you canker-blossom! [1]
You thief of love! what, have you come by night
And stol'n my love's heart from him?

HELENA.

                        Fine, i'faith!
Have you no modesty, no maiden shame,
No touch of bashfulness? What, will you tear
Impatient answers from my gentle tongue?
Fie, fie! you counterfeit, you puppet, [2] you!

HERMIA.

Puppet! why, so; ay, that way goes the game.
Now I perceive that she hath made compare
Between our statures; she hath urged her height;
And with her personage, her tall personage,
Her height, forsooth, she hath prevail'd with him.
And are you grown so high in his esteem,
Because I am so dwarfish and so low?
How low am I, thou painted maypole? speak;
How low am I? I am not yet so low
But that my nails can reach unto thine eyes.

HELENA.

I pray you, though you mock me, gentlemen,
Let her not hurt me: I was never curst; [3]
I have no gift at all in shrewishness;
I am a right maid [4] for my cowardice:
Let her not strike me. You perhaps may think,
Because she is something lower than myself,
That I can match her.

---

[1] **canker-blossom**: wild rose or dog rose; a term of derision as being inferior to the cultivated rose.
[2] **you counterfeit, you puppet**: in other words, you poor excuse for a woman.
[3] **curst**: shrewish; quarrelsome.
[4] **right maid**: true maid.

HERMIA.

Lower! hark, again.

HELENA.

Good Hermia, do not be so bitter with me.
I evermore[1] did love you, Hermia,
Did ever keep your counsels,[2] never wrong'd you;
Save that, in love unto Demetrius,
I told him of your stealth[3] unto this wood,
He follow'd you; for love I follow'd him;
But he hath chid me hence, and threaten'd me
To strike me, spurn me, nay, to kill me too:
And now, so you will let me quiet go,
To Athens will I bear my folly back,
And follow you no further: let me go:
You see how simple and how fond[4] I am.

HERMIA.

Why, get you gone: who is't that hinders you?

HELENA.

A foolish heart, that I leave here behind.

HERMIA.

What, with Lysander?

HELENA.

With Demetrius.

LYSANDER.

Be not afraid; she shall not harm thee, Helena.

DEMETRIUS.

No, sir, she shall not, though you take her part.

HELENA.

O, when she's angry, she is keen and shrewd![5]
She was a vixen when she went to school;
And though she be but little, she is fierce.

HERMIA.

Little again! nothing but low and little!—

---

[1] evermore: always.
[2] counsels: secrets; confidences.
[3] stealth: stealing.
[4] fond: foolish.
[5] keen and shrewd: cutting and shrewish.

Why will you suffer her to flout[1] me thus?
Let me come to her.

LYSANDER.

Get you gone, you dwarf;
You minimus,[2] of hind'ring knot-grass[3] made;
You bead, you acorn.

DEMETRIUS.

You are too officious
In her behalf that scorns your services.
Let her alone: speak not of Helena;
Take not her part; for, if thou dost intend
Never so little show of love to her,
Thou shalt aby it.[4]

LYSANDER.

Now she holds me not;
Now follow, if thou darest, to try whose right,
Of thine or mine, is most in Helena.

DEMETRIUS.

Follow! nay, I'll go with thee, cheek by jole.[5]

[*Exeunt* LYSANDER *and* DEMETRIUS.

HERMIA.

You, mistress, all this coil is 'long of you:[6]
Nay, go not back.

HELENA.

I will not trust you, I,
Nor longer stay in your curst company,
Your hands than mine are quicker for a fray;
My legs are longer though, to run away.   [*Exit.*

HERMIA.

I am amazed, and know not what to say.   [*Exit.*

OBERON.

This is thy negligence: still thou mistakest,
Or else committ'st thy knaveries wilfully.

---

[1] **flout:** mock. [2] **minimus:** insignificant thing. [3] **hind'ring knot-grass:** knotgrass was supposed to stunt the growth of those that ate it. [4] **aby it:** pay for it. [5] **cheek by jole:** cheek by jowl, as we say it today. [6] **all this coil is 'long of you:** all this turmoil, or trouble, is because of you.

PUCK.

Believe me, king of shadows, I mistook.
Did not you tell me I should know the man
By the Athenian garments he had on?
And so far blameless proves my enterprise,
That I have 'nointed an Athenian's eyes;
And so far am I glad it so did sort,[1]
As this their jangling I esteem a sport.

OBERON.

Thou see'st these lovers seek a place to fight:
Hie therefore, Robin, overcast the night;
The starry welkin[2] cover thou anon
With drooping fog, as black as Acheron;[3]
And lead these testy rivals so astray,
As one come not within another's[4] way.
Like to Lysander sometime frame thy tongue,
Then stir Demetrius up with bitter wrong;
And sometime rail thou like Demetrius;
And from each other look thou lead them thus,
Till o'er their brows death-counterfeiting sleep
With leaden legs and batty wings doth creep:
Then crush this herb into Lysander's eye;
Whose liquor[5] hath this virtuous property,
To take from thence all error with his might,[6]
And make his eyeballs roll with wonted [7] sight.
When they next wake, all this derision
Shall seem a dream and fruitless vision;
And back to Athens shall the lovers wend,
With league[8] whose date[9] till death shall never end.
Whiles I in this affair do thee employ,
I'll to my queen and beg her Indian boy;
And then I will her charmed eye release
From monster's view, and all things shall be peace.

---

[1] **it so did sort**: it turned out this way. [2] **welkin**: sky. [3] **Acheron**: a river in Hades, but often applied to hell itself. [4] **another's**: the other's. [5] **liquor**: juice. [6] **his might**: its power. [7] **wonted**: usual. [8] **league**: vows; ties. [9] **date**: duration.

PUCK.

My fairy lord, this must be done with haste,
For Night's swift dragons cut the clouds full fast,
And yonder shines Aurora's harbinger,[1]
At whose approach, ghosts, wandering here and there,
Troop home to churchyards: damned spirits all,
That in crossways and floods have burial,[2]
Already to their wormy beds are gone;
For fear lest day should look their shames upon,
They wilfully themselves exile from light,
And must for aye consort with black-brow'd night.

OBERON.

But we are spirits of another sort:
I with the Morning's love[3] have oft made sport;
And, like a forester, the groves may tread,
Even till the eastern gate, all fiery-red,
Opening on Neptune,[4] with fair blessed beams
Turns into yellow gold his salt green streams.
But, notwithstanding, haste; make no delay:
We may effect this business yet ere day.   [*Exit.*

PUCK.

                Up and down, up and down,
                I will lead them up and down:
                I am fear'd in field and town:
                Goblin, lead them up and down.

Here comes one.

Enter LYSANDER.

LYSANDER.

Where art thou, proud Demetrius? speak thou now.

---

[1] **Aurora's harbinger:** the morning star.
[2] **That in crossways and floods have burial:** unshriven souls of suicides and those drowned at sea who lie in unhallowed ground.
[3] **Morning's love:** Cephalus, whom the goddess Aurora loved.
[4] **Neptune:** the ocean, Neptune's realm.

PUCK.

Here, villain; drawn[1] and ready. Where art thou?

LYSANDER.

I will be with thee straight.[2]

PUCK.

Follow me, then,

To plainer ground.

[*Exit* LYSANDER, *as following the voice.*
Enter DEMETRIUS.

DEMETRIUS.

Lysander! speak agen.[3]

Thou runaway, thou coward, art thou fled?

Speak! in some bush? where dost thou hide thy head?

PUCK.

Thou coward, art thou bragging to the stars,

Telling the bushes that thou look'st for wars,

And wilt not come? Come, recreant;[4] come, thou child;

I'll whip thee with a rod: he is defiled

That draws a sword on thee.

DEMETRIUS.

Yea, art thou there?

PUCK.

Follow my voice: we'll try no manhood here.[5]   [*Exeunt.*
Enter LYSANDER.

LYSANDER.

He goes before me and still dares me on:

When I come where he calls, then he is gone.

The villain is much lighter-heel'd than I:

I follow'd fast, but faster he did fly;

That fall'n am I in dark uneven way,

---

[1] **drawn**: with sword drawn.
[2] **straight**: immediately.
[3] **agen**: again.
[4] **recreant**: coward.
[5] **we'll try no manhood here**: that is, we shall not test their courage here.

And here will rest me. [*Lies down.*] Come, thou gentle day!
For if but once thou show me thy gray light,
I'll find Demetrius, and revenge this spite.   [*Sleeps.*

Enter PUCK *and* DEMETRIUS.

PUCK.

Ho, ho, ho! Coward, why comest thou not?

DEMETRIUS.

Abide me,[1] if thou darest; for well I wot[2]
Thou runn'st before me, shifting every place,
And darest not stand, nor look me in the face.
Where art thou now?

PUCK.

              Come hither: I am here.

DEMETRIUS.

Nay, then, thou mock'st me. Thou shalt buy this dear,[3]
If ever I thy face by daylight see:
Now, go thy way. Faintness constraineth me
To measure out my length on this cold bed.
By day's approach look to be visited.

                    [*Lies down and sleeps.*

Enter HELENA.

HELENA.

O weary night, O long and tedious night,
    Abate[4] thy hours! Shine comforts from the east,
That I may back to Athens by daylight,
    From these that my poor company detest:
And sleep, that sometime shuts up sorrow's eye,
Steal me awhile from mine own company.

                    [*Lies down and sleeps.*

---

[1] **Abide me:** wait for me.
[2] **wot:** know.
[3] **buy this dear:** pay dearly for this.
[4] **Abate:** shorten or lessen.

PUCK.

Yet but three? Come one more;
Two of both kinds makes up four.
Here she comes, curst and sad:—
Cupid is a knavish lad,
Thus to make poor females mad.

Enter HERMIA.

HERMIA.

Never so weary, never so in woe;
  Bedabbled with the dew, and torn with briers;
I can no further crawl, no further go;
  My legs can keep no pace with my desires.
Here will I rest me till the break of day.
Heavens shield Lysander, if they mean a fray!

[*Lies down and sleeps.*

PUCK.

On the ground
Sleep sound:
I'll apply
To your eye,
Gentle lover, remedy.

[*Squeezing the herb on* LYSANDER'S *eyelids.*

When thou wakest,
Thou takest
True delight
In the sight
Of thy former lady's eye:
And the country proverb known,
That every man should take his own,
In your waking shall be shown:

Jack shall have Jill;[1]
Naught shall go ill;

The man shall have his mare again, and all shall be well. [*Exit.*

---

[1] "Jack shall have Jill": from Heywood's *Epigrammes* upon *Proverbes* (1567).

A
Midsummer
Night's Dream

ACT 4

ACT IV

OBERON, who in the meantime has won the boy he wants from Titania, now finds her and Bottom asleep in each other's arms. He applies to her eyes an antidote to the magic juice and she awakens to find her erstwhile beloved of the ass's head no longer desirable. The king and queen are reconciled as Theseus, his bride, and their attendants, accompanied by Egeus, appear as the sun rises. The four lovers, who have also been sleeping nearby, are wakened, Lysander now in love with Hermia once more and Demetrius with Helena. Though this is not the pairing-off that Egeus had demanded, it so pleases Theseus that he decrees that this shall be the resolution to the troubled affair, and invites the two now loving couples to be married on his wedding day. Bottom, who had slept on, now wakens with memories of a very strange dream, but sets out to join his fellows, who have given him up for lost. The act closes with the rustics, now joined by Bottom, preparing to perform their "most lamentable comedy" for Theseus and Hippolyta.

ACT IV. Scene I.

The wood. LYSANDER, DEMETRIUS, HELENA, *and* HERMIA, *lying asleep.*

Enter TITANIA *and* BOTTOM; PEAS-BLOSSOM, COBWEB, MOTH, MUSTARD-SEED, *and other* FAIRIES *attending;* OBERON *behind unseen.*

TITANIA.
Come, sit thee down upon this flowery bed,
   While I thy amiable[1] cheeks do coy,[2]
And stick musk-roses in thy sleek smooth head,
   And kiss thy fair large ears, my gentle joy.
BOTTOM.
Where's Peas-blossom?
PEAS-BLOSSOM.
Ready.
BOTTOM.
Scratch my head, Peas-blossom.—Where's Monsieur Cobweb?
COBWEB.
Ready.
BOTTOM.
Monsieur Cobweb, good monsieur, get your weapons in your hand, and kill me a red-hipt humble-bee on the top of a thistle; and, good monsieur, bring me the honey-bag. Do not fret yourself too much in the action, monsieur; and, good monsieur, have a care the honey-bag break not; I would be loth to have you overflown[3] with a honey-bag, signior.— Where's Monsieur Mustard-seed?

---

[1] **amiable:** pleasing; lovable.
[2] **coy:** caress.
[3] **overflown:** overflowed or covered.

MUSTARD-SEED.

Ready.

BOTTOM.

Give me your neif, Monsieur Mustard-seed. Pray you, leave
your courtesy, good monsieur.

MUSTARD-SEED.

What's your will?

BOTTOM.

Nothing, good monsieur, but to help Cavalery[1] Peas-blossom
to scratch. I must to the barber's, monsieur; for methinks I
am marvellous hairy about the face; and I am such a tender
ass, if my hair do but tickle me, I must scratch.

TITANIA.

What, wilt thou hear some music, my sweet love?

BOTTOM.

I have a reasonable good ear in music: let's have the tongs
and bones.[2]   [*Tongs. Rural music.*

TITANIA.

Or say, sweet love, what thou desirest to eat.

BOTTOM.

Truly, a peck of provender: I could munch your good dry
oats. Methinks I have a great desire to a bottle of hay;[3] good
hay, sweet hay hath no fellow.[4]

TITANIA.

I have a venturous fairy that shall seek
The squirrel's hoard, and fetch thee hence new nuts.

BOTTOM.

I had rather have a handful or two of dried peas.

---

[1] **Cavalery:** Cavalero.
[2] **the tongs and bones:** crude musical instruments used in rural areas.
[3] **bottle of hay:** truss of hay.
[4] **fellow:** equal.

But, I pray you, let none of your people stir me:
I have an exposition of[1] sleep come upon me.

> TITANIA.

Sleep thou, and I will wind thee in my arms.—
Fairies, be gone, and be all ways[2] away.—

[Exeunt FAIRIES.

So doth the woodbine the sweet honeysuckle
Gently entwist; the female ivy so
Enrings the barky fingers of the elm.
O, how I love thee! how I dote on thee!   *[They sleep.*

> *Enter* PUCK.
> OBERON [*advancing*].

Welcome, good Robin. See'st thou this sweet sight?
Her dotage[3] now I do begin to pity:
For, meeting her of late behind the wood,
Seeking sweet favours[4] for this hateful fool,
I did upbraid her, and fall out with her;
For she his hairy temples then had rounded
With coronet of fresh and fragrant flowers;
And that same dew, which sometime on the buds
Was wont[5] to swell, like round and orient pearls,
Stood now within the pretty flowerets'[6] eyes,
Like tears, that did their own disgrace bewail.
When I had at my pleasure taunted her,
And she in mild terms begg'd my patience,
I then did ask of her her changeling child;
Which straight[7] she gave me, and her fairy sent
To bear him to my bower in fairy-land.
And now I have the boy, I will undo
This hateful imperfection[8] of her eyes:
And, gentle Puck, take this transformed scalp

---

[1] **exposition of:** disposition for (another of Bottom's malapropisms).
[2] **all ways:** in all directions. [3] **dotage:** doting affection. [4] **favours:** love tokens. [5] **wont:** accustomed. [6] **flowerets:** little flowers. [7] **straight:** immediately. [8] **imperfection:** disorder.

From off the head of this Athenian swain;
That he, awaking when the other do,
May all to Athens back again repair,[1]
And think no more of this night's accidents,[2]
But[3] as the fierce[4] vexation of a dream.
But first I will release the fairy queen.
     Be as thou wast wont to be;
        [Touching her eyes with an herb.
     See as thou wast wont to see:
     Dian's bud [5] o'er Cupid's flower
     Hath such force and blessed power.
Now, my Titania: wake you, my sweet queen.
 TITANIA.
My Oberon! what visions have I seen!
Methought I was enamour'd of an ass.
 OBERON.
There lies your love.
 TITANIA.
     How came these things to pass?
O, how mine eyes do loathe his visage now!
 OBERON.
Silence awhile.—Robin, take off this head.—
Titania, music call; and strike more dead
Than common sleep of all these five the sense.
 TITANIA.
Music, ho! music, such as charmeth sleep!
         [Music, still.
 PUCK.
Now, when thou wakest, with thine own fool's eyes peep.
 OBERON.
Sound, music!—Come, my queen, take hands with me,

---

[1] **repair**: return.
[2] **accidents**: incidents.
[3] **But**: except.
[4] **fierce**: wild; disordered.
[5] **Dian's bud**: an allusion to Diana as the chaste goddess.

And rock the ground whereon these sleepers be.
Now thou and I are new in amity,
And will to-morrow midnight solemnly[1]
Dance in Duke Theseus' house triumphantly,
And bless it to all fair prosperity:
There shall the pairs of faithful lovers be
Wedded, with Theseus, all in jollity.

PUCK.
                    Fairy king, attend, and mark:
                    I do hear the morning lark.

OBERON.
                    Then, my queen, in silence sad,
                    Trip we after the night's shade:
                    We the globe can compass soon,
                    Swifter than the wandering moon.

TITANIA.
                    Come, my lord; and in our flight,
                    Tell me how it came this night
                    That I sleeping here was found
                    With these mortals on the ground.

                            [*Exeunt. Wind horns.*

            Enter THESEUS, HIPPOLYTA, EGEUS, *and* TRAIN.

THESEUS.
Go, one of you, find out the forester;
For now our observation[2] is perform'd;
And since we have the vaward [3] of the day,
My love shall hear the music of my hounds:
Uncouple[4] in the western valley; go:—
Dispatch,[5] I say, and find the forester.—

                            [*Exit an* ATTENDANT.
We will, fair queen, up to the mountain's top,

---

[1] **solemnly:** with due ceremony; ceremoniously.
[2] **observation:** observation of May Day.
[3] **vaward:** vanguard; beginning.
[4] **Uncouple:** loose.
[5] **Dispatch:** hurry.

And mark the musical confusion
Of hounds and echo in conjunction.

HIPPOLYTA.

I was with Hercules and Cadmus[1] once,
When in a wood of Crete they bay'd [2] the bear
With hounds of Sparta: never did I hear
Such gallant chiding; for besides the groves
The skies, the fountains, every region near
Seem all one mutual cry: I never heard
So musical a discord, such sweet thunder.

THESEUS.

My hounds are bred out of the Spartan kind,
So flew'd, so sanded;[3] and their heads are hung
With ears that sweep away the morning dew;
Crook-knee'd, and dew-lapt like Thessalian bulls
Slow in pursuit, but matcht in mouth like bells,
Each under each. A cry more tuneable[4]
Was never holla'd to, nor cheer'd with horn,
In Crete, in Sparta, nor in Thessaly:
Judge when you hear.—But, soft! [5] what nymphs are these?

EGEUS.

My lord, this is my daughter here asleep
And this, Lysander; this Demetrius is;
This Helena, old Nedar's Helena:
I wonder of their being here together.

THESEUS.

No doubt they rose up early to observe
The rites of May; and, hearing our intent,
Came here in grace[6] of our solemnity.—
But speak, Egeus; is not this the day
That Hermia should give answer of her choice?

---

[1] **Cadmus:** son of Agenor, King of Phoenicia, brother of Europa, and founder of Thebes and the race of men known as Sparti. [2] **bay'd:** brought to bay. [3] **So flew'd, so sanded:** having the same folds of fleshy skin around the jaws and the same sandy color as the Cretan hounds: the dogs of Sparta and Crete were famed for their hunting instincts. [4] **tuneable:** tuneful. [5] **soft:** wait; hold on. [6] **grace:** honor.

EGEUS.

It is, my lord.

THESEUS.

Go, bid the huntsmen wake them with their horns.

[*Horns, and they wake. Shout within, and they all start up.*

Good morrow, friends.—Saint Valentine is past:

Begin these wood-birds but to couple now?[1]

LYSANDER.

Pardon, my lord.

THESEUS.

I pray you all, stand up.

I know you two are rival enemies:

How comes this gentle concord in the world,

That hatred is so far from jealousy,[2]

To sleep by hate,[3] and fear no enmity?

LYSANDER.

My lord, I shall reply amazedly,

Half sleep, half waking: but as yet, I swear,

I cannot truly say how I came here;

But, as I think,—for truly would I speak,

And now I do bethink me, so it is,—

I came with Hermia hither: our intent

Was to be gone from Athens, where we might

Without the peril of the Athenian law,—

EGEUS.

Enough, enough, my lord; you have enough:

I beg the law, the law, upon his head.—

They would have stol'n away; they would, Demetrius,

Thereby to have defeated you and me,

You of your wife, and me of my consent,—

Of my consent that she should be your wife.

---

[1] **to couple now**: only to mate now.

[2] **jealousy**: suspicion.

[3] **To sleep by hate**: as to sleep beside hate.

DEMETRIUS.

My lord, fair Helen told me of their stealth,
Of this their purpose hither to this wood;
And I in fury hither follow'd them,
Fair Helena in fancy[1] following me.
But, my good lord, I wot[2] not by what power,—
But by some power it is,—my love to Hermia,
Melted as the snow, seems to me now
As the remembrance of an idle gaud,[3]
Which in my childhood I did dote upon;
And all the faith, the virtue of my heart,
The object, and the pleasure of mine eye,
Is only Helena. To her, my lord,
Was I betroth'd ere I saw Hermia:
But, like in sickness,[4] did I loathe this food;
But, as in health, come[5] to my natural taste,
Now do I wish it, love it, long for it,
And will for evermore be true to it.

THESEUS.

Fair lovers, you are fortunately met:
Of this discourse we more will hear anon.—
Egeus, I will overbear[6] your will;
For in the temple, by and by, with us
These couples shall eternally be knit.[7]
And, for the morning now is something worn,
Our purposed hunting shall be set aside.
Away with us to Athens! three and three,
We'll hold a feast in great solemnity.
Come, Hippolyta.

[*Exeunt* THESEUS, HIPPOLYTA, EGEUS, *and* TRAIN.

DEMETRIUS.

These things seem small and undistinguishable,

---

[1] **in fancy:** because of love. [2] **wot:** know. [3] **gawd:** trifle; toy; something with which to while away the time. [4] **in sickness:** a person sick. [5] **come:** having returned. [6] **overbear:** overrule. [7] **be knit:** be united.

Like far-off mountains turned into clouds.

HERMIA.

Methinks I see these things with parted eye,
When everything seems double.

HELENA.

So methinks:
And I have found Demetrius like a gemel,[1]
Mine own, and not mine own.[2]

DEMETRIUS.

Are you sure
That we are awake? It seems to me
That yet we sleep, we dream.—Do not you think
The duke was here, and bid us follow him?

HERMIA.

Yea; and my father.

HELENA.

And Hippolyta.

LYSANDER.

And he did bid us follow to the temple.

DEMETRIUS.

Why, then, we are awake: let's follow him;
And, by the way, let us recount our dreams.   [*Exeunt.*

BOTTOM [*awaking*].

When my cue comes, call me, and I will answer:—my next is,
'Most fair Pyramus,'——Heigh-ho!—Peter Quince! Flute the
bellows-mender! Snout the tinker! Starveling!—God's my life,
stol'n hence, and left me asleep! I have had a most rare vision.
I have had a dream,—past the wit of man to say what dream
it was: man is but an ass, if he go about[3] to expound this
dream. Methought I was—there is no man can tell what.
Methought I was, and methought I had,—but man is but a

---

[1] gemel: jewel.
[2] Mine own, and not mine own: in my possession, but subject to
claim by another.
[3] go about: attempt.

patcht[1] fool, if he will offer to say what methought I had. The
eye of man hath not heard,[2] the ear of man hath not seen,
man's hand is not able to taste, his tongue to conceive, nor
his heart to report, what my dream was. I will get Peter
Quince to write a ballet[3] of this dream: it shall be called Bottom's Dream, because it hath no bottom; and I will sing it in
the latter end of a play before the duke: peradventure, to
make it the more gracious, I shall sing it at her death.

[*Exit.*

SCENE II.

Athens. A room in QUINCE'S *house.*

Enter QUINCE, FLUTE, SNOUT, *and* STARVELING.

QUINCE.
Have you sent to Bottom's house? is he come home yet?
    STARVELING.
He cannot be heard of. Out of doubt[4] he is transported.[5]
    FLUTE.
If he come not, then the play is marr'd:[6] it goes not forward,
doth it?
    QUINCE.
It is not possible: you have not a man in all Athens able to
discharge Pyramus but he.
    FLUTE.
No, he hath simply the best wit of any handicraft man in
Athens.
    QUINCE.
Yea, and the best person too; and he is a very paramour for a

---

[1] **pacht:** a reference to the patched clothing (motley) of the court
fool. [2] **The eye of man hath not heard, etc.:** a jumbled version of
1 Corinthians 2:9. [3] **ballet:** ballad. [4] **Out of doubt:** beyond doubt.
[5] **transported:** carried off, perhaps killed. [6] **marr'd:** ruined.

sweet voice.

FLUTE.

You must say paragon: a paramour is, God bless us, a thing
of naught.[1]

Enter SNUG.

SNUG.

Masters, the duke is coming from the temple, and there is[2]
two or three lords and ladies more married: if our sport had
gone forward, we had all been made men.

FLUTE.

O sweet bully Bottom! Thus hath he lost sixpence a day during his life; he could not have scaped sixpence a day: an the[3]
duke had not given him sixpence a day for playing Pyramus,
I'll be hang'd; he would have deserved it: sixpence a day in
Pyramus, or nothing.

Enter BOTTOM.

BOTTOM.

Where are these lads? where are these hearts?[4]

QUINCE.

Bottom!—O most courageous day! O most happy hour!

BOTTOM.

Masters, I am to discourse wonders: but ask me not what; for
if I tell you, I am no true Athenian. I will tell you everything,
right[5] as it fell out.

QUINCE.

Let us hear, sweet Bottom.

BOTTOM.

Not a word of me.[6] All that I will tell you is, that the duke

---

[1] **a thing of naught:** a naughty or wicked thing.
[2] **is:** are.
[3] **an the:** if the.
[4] **hearts:** a familiar form of address; hearties.
[5] **right:** exactly.
[6] **of me:** from me.

hath dined. Get your apparel together good strings[1] to your beards, new ribbons to your pumps; meet presently at the palace; every man look o'er his part; for the short and the long is, our play is preferr'd.[2] In any case, let Thisby have clean linen; and let not him that plays the lion pare his nails, for they shall hang out for the lion's claws. And, most dear actors, eat no onions nor garlic, for we are to utter sweet breath; and I do not doubt but to hear them say it is a sweet comedy. No more words; away! go; away!

[*Exeunt.*

---

[1] **strings:** ties for false beards.
[2] **preferr'd:** offered for approval.

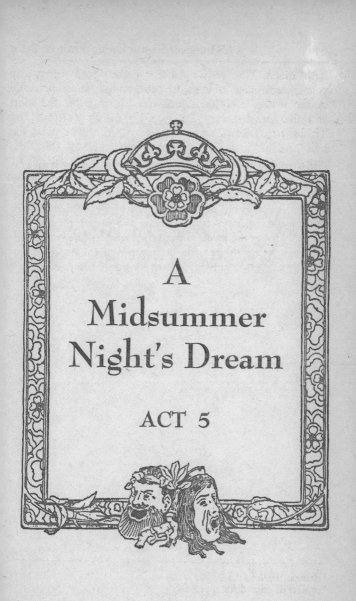

A
Midsummer
Night's Dream

ACT 5

ACT V

THE STORY of the play is now over, and the last act is an epilogue. It consists of the rustics' play, which all enjoy, though it evokes some varied comment from the spectators, followed by a rustic dance, or "Bergomask." The newly wedded couples retire, while the fairies come dancing and singing through the palace, blessing the lovers and their marriages. They dance off and Puck is left to crave the indulgence of the audience for the unusual performance that they have just witnessed.

ACT V. SCENE I.

Athens. An apartment in the palace of THESEUS.

Enter THESEUS, HIPPOLYTA, PHILOSTRATE, LORDS, *and*
ATTENDANTS.

HIPPOLYTA.
'Tis strange, my Theseus, that these lovers speak of.
THESEUS.
More strange than true: I never may[1] believe
These antick[2] fables nor these fairy toys.[3]
Lovers and madmen have such seething brains,
Such shaping fantasies,[4] that apprehend
More than cool reason ever comprehends.
The lunatic, the lover, and the poet
Are of imagination all compact:[5]—
One sees more devils than vast hell can hold,—
That is, the madman: the lover, all as frantic,
Sees Helen's beauty in a brow of Egypt:[6]
The poet's eye, in a fine frenzy rolling,
Doth glance from heaven to earth, from earth to heaven;
And, as imagination bodies forth

---

[1] may: can. [2] antick: antique. [3] toys: trifles. [4] fantasies: fancies.
[5] Are of imagination all compact: are made up, or composed, of
imagination. [6] a brow of Egypt: a gypsy, or dark, beauty.

The forms of things unknown, the poet's pen
Turns them to shapes, and gives to airy nothing
A local habitation and a name.
Such tricks hath strong imagination,
That, if it would but apprehend [1] some joy,
It comprehends[2] some bringer of that joy;
Or in the night, imagining some fear,
How easy is a bush supposed a bear!

HIPPOLYTA.

But all the story of the night told over,
And all their minds transfigured so together,
More witnesseth than fancy's images,[3]
And grows to something of great constancy;[4]
But, howsoever, strange and admirable.

THESEUS.

Here come the lovers, full of joy and mirth.

    Enter LYSANDER, DEMETRIUS, HERMIA, *and* HELENA.

Joy, gentle friends! joy and fresh days of love
Accompany your hearts!

LYSANDER.

                   More than to us
Wait in your royal walks, your board, your bed!

THESEUS.

Come now; what masks, what dances shall we have,
To wear away this long age of three hours
Between our after-supper[5] and bed-time?
Where is our usual manager of mirth?
What revels are in hand? Is there no play,
To ease the anguish of a torturing hour?
Call Philostrate.

---

[1] apprehend: conceive. [2] comprehends: also includes. [3] More witnesseth than fancy's images: attest to more than mere images of fancy. [4] constancy: consistency. [5] our after-supper: Schmidt says Shakespeare means the time after supper.

PHILOSTRATE.
                    Here, mighty Theseus.
    THESEUS.
Say, what abridgement[1] have you for this evening?
What mask? what music? How shall we beguile
The lazy time, if not with some delight?
    PHILOSTRATE.
There is a brief how many[2] sports are ripe:[3]
Make choice of which your highness will see first.

                                        [*Giving a paper.*

                    THESEUS [*reads*].
'The battle with the Centaurs,[4] to be sung
By an Athenian eunuch to the harp.'
We'll none of that: that have I told my love,
In glory of my kinsman Hercules.—
[*Reads*] 'The riot of the tipsy Bacchanals,
Tearing the Thracian singer[5] in their rage.'
That is an old device; and it was play'd
When I from Thebes came last a conqueror.—
[*Reads*] 'The thrice-three Muses mourning for the death
Of Learning, late deceased in beggary.'
That is some satire, keen and critical,
Not sorting with a nuptial ceremony.[6]—
[*Reads*] 'A tedious brief scene of young Pyramus
And his love Thisbe; very tragical mirth.'
Merry and tragical! tedious and brief!
That is, hot ice and wondrous strange snow.
How shall we find the concord of this discord?
    PHILOSTRATE.
A play there is, my lord, some ten words long,
Which is as brief as I have known a play;
But by ten words, by lord, it is too long,
Which makes it tedious; for in all the play

---

[1] abridgement: pastime. [2] brief how many: list of how many. [3] ripe:
ready. "The battle with the Centaurs': the battle of the Centaurs
and the Lapithae, a favorite subject with the poets and sculptors of
antiquity. [5] the Thracian singer: Orpheus was killed by the Thracian
women during a riot while celebrating the orgies of Bacchus. [6] not
sorting with a nuptial ceremony: not in keeping with the spirit
of a wedding.

There is not one word apt, one player fitted:
And tragical, my noble lord, it is;
For Pyramus therein doth kill himself.
Which, when I saw rehearsed, I must confess,
Made mine eyes water; but more merry tears
The passion of loud laughter never shed.

THESEUS.

What are they that do play it?

PHILOSTRATE.

Hard-handed men,[1] that work in Athens here,
Which never labour'd in their minds till now;
And now have toil'd [2] their unbreathed memories[3]
With this same play, against your nuptial.

THESEUS.

And we will hear it.

PHILOSTRATE.

          No, my noble lord;
It is not for you: I have heard it over,
And it is nothing, nothing in the world;
Unless you can find sport in their intents,
Extremely stretcht[4] and conn'd with cruel pain,[5]
To do you service.

THESEUS.

          I will hear that play;
For never any thing can be amiss,
When simpleness and duty tender it.
Go, bring them in:—and take your places, ladies.

                   [*Exit* PHILOSTRATE.

HIPPOLYTA.

I love not to see wretchedness o'ercharged,[6]
And duty in his service[7] perishing.

THESEUS.

Why, gentle sweet, you shall see no such thing.

---

[1] **Hard-handed men:** laboring men. [2] **toil'd:** strained. [3] **unbreathed memories:** inexperienced minds. [4] **stretcht:** strained; affected. [5] **conn'd with cruel pain:** memorized with great effort. [6] **wretchedness o'er-charged:** the poor overtaxed. [7] **his service:** its service.

HIPPOLYTA.

He says they can do nothing in this kind.

THESEUS.

The kinder we, to give them thanks for nothing.
Our sport shall be to take what they mistake:[1]
And what poor duty cannot do,
Noble respect takes it in might, not merit.[2]
Where I have come,[3] great clerks have purposed
To greet me with premeditated welcomes;
Where I have seen them shiver and look pale,
Make periods[4] in the midst of sentences,
Throttle their practised accent in their fears,
And, in conclusion, dumbly have broke off,
Not paying me a welcome. Trust me, sweet,
Out of this silence yet I pickt a welcome;
And in the modesty of fearful duty[5]
I read as much as from the rattling tongue
Of saucy and audacious eloquence.
Love, therefore, and tongue-tied simplicity,
In least speak most, to my capacity.[6]

Enter PHILOSTRATE.

PHILOSTRATE.

So please your grace, the Prologue is addrest.[7]

THESEUS.

Let him approach.   [*Flourish of trumpets.*
Enter the PROLOGUE.

PROLOGUE.

If we offend, it is with our good will.
    That you should think, we come not to offend,
But with good will. To show our simple skill,
    That is the true beginning of our end.[8]
Consider, then, we come but in despite.

---

[1] **to take what they mistake:** to accept their blunders. [2] **Noble respect takes it in might, not merit:** a noble mind takes into account the effort expended in the performance, not the merit of the performance. [3] **come:** traveled. [4] **periods:** come to a stop. [5] **modesty of fearful duty:** the shyness of one performing a dreaded but necessary duty. [6] **to my capacity:** in my understanding. [7] **addrest:** ready. [8] **end:** aim.

We do not come as minding to content you,[1]
Our true intent is. All for your delight,
We are not here. That you should here repent you,
The actors are at hand; and, by their show,
You shall know all that you are like to know.

THESEUS.

This fellow doth not stand upon points.

LYSANDER.

He hath rid [2] his prologue like a rough colt; he knows not the stop. A good moral, my lord: it is not enough to speak, but to speak true.

HIPPOLYTA.

Indeed he hath play'd on his prologue like a child on a recorder,[3] a sound, but not in government.[4]

THESEUS.

His speech was like a tangled chain; nothing impair'd, but all disorder'd. Who is next?

Enter PYRAMUS *and* THISBE, WALL, MOONSHINE, *and* LION.

PROLOGUE.

Gentles,[5] perchance you wonder at this show;
    But wonder on, till truth make all things plain.
This man is Pyramus, if you would know;
    This beauteous lady, Thisbe is certain.
This man, with lime and rough-cast, doth present[6]
    Wall, that vile Wall which did these lovers sunder;
And through Wall's chink, poor souls, they are content
    To whisper; at the which let no man wonder.

---

[1] **as minding to content you:** with the idea of pleasing you in mind. [2] **rid:** ridden. [3] **recorder:** flageolet (flute). [4] **not in government:** not under control. [5] **Gentles:** a form of address to an audience, equivalent to "ladies and gentlemen." [6] **present:** represent.

This man, with lantern, dog, and bush of thorn,
   Presenteth Moonshine; for, if you will know
By moonshine did these lovers think no scorn
   To meet at Ninus' tomb, there, there to woo
This grisly[1] beast, which by name Lion hight,[2]
The trusty Thisbe, coming first by night,
Did scare away, or rather did affright;
And, as she fled, her mantle she did fall,
   Which Lion vile with bloody mouth did stain.
Anon comes Pyramus, sweet youth and tall,
   And finds his trusty Thisbe's mantle slain:
Whereat, with blade, with bloody blameful blade,
   He bravely broacht[3] his boiling bloody breast;
And Thisbe, tarrying in mulberry shade,
   His dagger drew,[4] and died. For all the rest,
Let Lion, Moonshine, Wall, and lovers twain,
At large[5] discourse, while here they do remain.
[*Exeunt* PROLOGUE, PYRAMUS, THISBE, LION, *and* MOONSHINE.

THESEUS.
I wonder if the lion be to speak.[6]

DEMETRIUS.
No wonder, my lord: one lion may, when many asses do.

WALL.
In this same interlude it doth befall
That I, one Snout by name, present a wall;
And such a wall, as I would have you think,
That had in it a crannied hole or chink,
Through which the lovers, Pyramus and Thisbe,

---

[1] grisly: terrible; grim.
[2] hight: is called.
[3] broacht: stabbed.
[4] drew: withdrew.
[5] At large: at length.
[6] if the lion be to speak: if the lion is able to talk.

Did whisper often very secretly.
This loam, this rough-cast, and this stone, doth show
That I am that same wall; the truth is so:
And this the cranny is, right and sinister,[1]
Through which the fearful [2] lovers are to whisper.

THESEUS.

Would you desire lime and hair to speak better?

DEMETRIUS.

It is the wittiest partition that ever I heard discourse, my lord.

THESEUS.

Pyramus draws near the wall: silence!

Enter PYRAMUS.

PYRAMUS.

O grim-lookt[3] night! O night with hue so black!
  O night, which ever art when day is not!
O night, O night! alack, alack, alack,
  I fear my Thisbe's promise is forgot!—
And thou, O wall, O sweet, O lovely wall,
  That stand'st between her father's ground and mine!
Thou wall, O wall, O sweet and lovely wall,
  Show me thy chink, to blink through with mine eyne!
                    [WALL *holds up his fingers.*
Thanks, courteous wall: Jove shield thee well for this!
  But what see I? No Thisbe do I see.
O wicked wall, through whom I see no bliss!
  Cursed be thy stones for thus deceiving me!

---

[1] **right and sinister:** right and left.
[2] **fearful:** frightened.
[3] **grim-lookt:** grim-looking.

THESEUS.

The wall, methinks, being sensible,[1] should curse again.[2]

BOTTOM.

No, in truth, sir, he should not. 'Deceiving me' is Thisbe's
cue: she is to enter now, and I am to spy her through the wall.
You shall see, it will fall pat[3] as I told you.—Yonder she
comes.

Enter THISBE.

THISBE.

O wall, full often hast thou heard my moans,
   For parting my fair Pyramus and me!
My cherry lips have often kist thy stones,
   Thy stones with lime and hair knit up in thee.

PYRAMUS.

I see a voice: now will I to the chink,
To spy an[4] I can hear[5] my Thisbe's face.—
Thisbe!

THISBE.

My love! thou art my love, I think.

PYRAMUS.

Think what thou wilt, I am thy lover's grace;
And, like Limander,[6] am I trusty still.

THISBE.

And I like Helen,[7] till the Fates me kill.

PYRAMUS.

Not Shafalus to Procrus[8] was so true.

THISBE.

As Shafalus to Procrus, I to you.

PYRAMUS.

O, kiss me through the hole of this vile wall!

THISBE.

I kiss the wall's hole, not your lips at all.

---

[1] **being sensible:** having perception or sense. [2] **again:** in return.
[3] **fall pat:** happen exactly. [4] **To spy an:** to see if. [5] **hear:** hear and see
are used indiscriminately, without regard to meaning. [6] **Limander:**
Leander, who swam the Hellespont every night to visit Hero.
[7] **Helen:** Hero. [8] **Shafalus to Procrus:** Cephalus to Procris; in Greek
Mythology, Cephalus was married to Procris, when Aurora saw him
and fell in love with him; he resisted all Aurora's attempts to win
him and at last she gave up.

PYRAMUS.

Wilt thou at Ninny's[1] tomb meet me straightway?

THISBE.

'Tide[2] life, 'tide death, I come without delay.

[Exeunt PYRAMUS *and* THISBE.

WALL.

Thus have I, wall, my part discharged so;

And, being done, thus wall away doth go.   *[Exit.*

THESEUS.

Now is the mural [3] down between the two neighbours.

DEMETRIUS.

No remedy, my lord, when walls are so wilful to hear without warning.

HIPPOLYTA.

This is the silliest stuff that e'er I heard.

THESEUS.

The best in this kind [4] are but shadows; and the worst are no worse, if imagination amend them.

HIPPOLYTA.

It must be your imagination then, and not theirs.

THESEUS.

If we imagine no worse of them than they of themselves, they may pass for excellent men.—Here come two noble beasts in, a moon and a lion.

Enter LION *and* MOONSHINE.

LION.

You, ladies, you, whose gentle hearts do fear,

The smallest monstrous mouse that creeps on floor,

---

[1] Ninny: Ninus—see p. 45.
[2] 'Tide: betide; happen.
[3] mural: wall.
[4] The best in this kind: the best of plays.

May now perchance both quake and tremble here,
  When lion rough in wildest rage doth roar.
Then know that I one Snug the joiner am,
No lion fell, nor else no lion's dam;[1]
For, if I should as lion come in strife
Into this place, 'twere pity on my life.

    THESEUS.
A very gentle beast, and of a good conscience.

    DEMETRIUS.
The very best at a beast, my lord, that e'er I saw.

    LYSANDER.
This lion is a very fox for his valour.[2]

    THESEUS.
True; and a goose[3] for his discretion.

    DEMETRIUS.
Not so, my lord; for his valour cannot carry his discretion; and
the fox carries the goose.

    THESEUS.
His discretion, I am sure, cannot carry his valour; for the
goose carries not the fox. It is well: leave it to his discretion,
and let us listen to the moon.

    MOONSHINE
This lantern doth the horned moon present;—

    DEMETRIUS.
He should have worn the horns on his head.

    THESEUS.
He is no crescent,[4] and his horns are invisible within the
circumference.

    MOONSHINE.
This lantern doth the horned moon present;[5]

---

[1] **No lion fell, nor else no lion's dam:** neither a lion's skin nor even a
lioness.
[2] **a very fox for his valour:** more cunning than brave.
[3] **goose:** fool.
[4] **no cresent:** that is, not a waxing moon.
[5] **present:** represent.

Myself the man-i-th'-moon do seem to be.

THESEUS.

This is the greatest error of all the rest: the man should be put into the lantern. How is it else the man-i'-th'-moon?

DEMETRIUS.

He dares not come there for the candle; for, you see, it is already in snuff.[1]

HIPPOLYTA.

I am a-weary of this moon: would he would change!

THESEUS.

It appears, by his small light of discretion, that he is in the wane; but yet, in courtesy, in all reason, we must stay[2] the time.

LYSANDER.

Proceed, moon.

MOONSHINE.

All that I have to say is, to tell you that the lantern is the moon; I, the man-i'-th'-moon; this thorn-bush, my thorn-bush; and this dog, my dog.

DEMETRIUS.

Why, all these should be in the lantern; for all these are in the moon. But, silence! here comes Thisbe.

Enter THISBE.

THISBE.

This is old Ninny's tomb. Where is my love?

O —   [*The* LION *roars;* THISBE *runs off.*

---

[1] **in snuff:** a common phrase for "in anger"; a pun.
[2] **stay:** await.

DEMETRIUS.
Well roar'd, lion.

THESEUS.
Well run, Thisbe.

HIPPOLYTA.
Well shone, moon.—Truly, the moon shines with a good
grace.

[*The* LION *tears* THISBE's *mantle, and exit.*

THESEUS.
Well moused, lion.

DEMETRIUS.
And then came Pyramus.

LYSANDER.
And so the lion vanisht.

Enter PYRAMUS.

PYRAMUS.
Sweet moon, I thank thee for thy sunny beams;
I thank thee, moon, for shining now so bright;
For, by thy gracious, golden, glittering streams,
I trust to taste of truest Thisbe's sight.
But stay,—O spite!—
But mark, poor knight,
What dreadful dole[1] is here!
Eyes, do you see?
How can it be?
O dainty duck! O dear!
Thy mantle good,
What, stain'd with blood?
Approach, ye Furies fell![2]
O Fates, come, come,
Cut thread and thrum;[3]
Quail, crush, conclude, and quell! [4]

---

[1] **dole**: grief.
[2] **fell**: deadly.
[3] **thrum**: fringe of woven thread.
[4] **quell**: destroy.

THESEUS.

This passion, and the death of a dear friend, would go near to
make a man look sad.

HIPPOLYTA.

Beshrew my heart, but I pity the man.

PYRAMUS.

O, wherefore, Nature, didst thou lions frame?
  Since lion vile hath here deflower'd my dear:
Which is—no, no—which was the fairest dame
    That lived, that loved, that liked, that lookt
        with cheer.[1]
                Come, tears, confound;[2]
                Out, sword, and wound
            The pap[3] of Pyramus,—
                Ay, that left pap,
                Where heart doth hop:—

                                            [Stabs himself.

            Thus die I, thus, thus, thus.
                Now am I dead,
                Now am I fled;
            My soul is in the sky:
                Tongue, lose thy light;
                Moon, take thy flight:—

                                [Exit MOONSHINE.
            Now die, die, die, die, die.   [Dies.

DEMETRIUS.

No die, but an ace,[4] for him; for he is but one.

LYSANDER.

Less than an ace, man; for he is dead; he is nothing.

---

[1] cheer: countenance.
[2] confound: confuse.
[3] pap: breast.
[4] No die, but an ace: Rolfe says this is an allusion to the spots on
dice.

THESEUS.

With the help of a surgeon he might yet recover; and prove
an ass.

HIPPOLYTA.

How chance[1] Moonshine is gone before Thisbe comes back
to find her lover?

THESEUS.

She will find him by starlight.—Here she comes, and her
passion ends the play.

Enter THISBE.

HIPPOLYTA.

Methinks she should not use a long one for such a Pyramus:
I hope she will be brief.

DEMETRIUS.

A mote will turn the balance, which Pyramus, which Thisbe,
is the better; he for a man, God warrant us,—she for a
woman, God bless us.

LYSANDER.

She hath spied him already with those sweet eyes.

DEMETRIUS.

And thus she moans, *videlicet:*[2]

THISBE.

> Asleep, my love?
>   What, dead, my dove?
> O Pyramus, arise!
>   Speak, speak. Quite dumb?
>   Dead, dead? A tomb
> Must cover thy sweet eyes.
>   These lily lips,
>   This cherry nose,
> These yellow cowslip cheeks,

---

[1] **How chance:** how does it happen.
[2] *videlicet:* viz; as follows.

Are gone, are gone:
    Lovers, make moan:[1]
His eyes were green as leeks.
    O Sisters Three,[2]
    Come, come to me,
With hands as pale as milk;
    Lay them in gore,
    Since you have shore[3]
With shears his thread of silk.
    Tongue, not a word:
    Come, trusty sword;
Come, blade, my breast imbrue;[4]

                                [Stabs herself.

    And, farewell, friends,—
    Thus Thisbe ends,—
    Adieu, adieu, adieu.   *[Dies.*

THESEUS.

Moonshine and Lion are left to bury the dead.

DEMETRIUS.

Ay, and Wall too.

BOTTOM.

No, I assure you; the wall is down that parted their fathers. Will it please you to see the epilogue, or to hear a Bergomask dance[5] between two of our company?

THESEUS.

No epilogue, I pray you; for your play needs no excuse. Never excuse; for when the players are all dead, there need none to be blamed. Marry, if he that writ it had play'd Pyramus and hang'd himself in Thisbe's garter, it would have been a fine tragedy: and so it is, truly; and very notably discharged. But,

---

[1] **make moan:** lament.
[2] **Sisters Three:** the three Fates.
[3] **shore:** used instead of shorn for the sake of the rhyme.
[4] **imbrue:** stain with blood.
[5] **a Bergomask dance:** a crude dance performed by the peasants of Bergomasco, a Venetian province.

come, your Bergomask: let your epilogue alone.   [A *dance.*
The iron tongue of midnight hath told twelve:—
Lovers, to bed; 'tis almost fairy-time.
I fear we shall out-sleep the coming morn,
As much as we this night have overwatcht.[1]
This papable-gross[2] play hath well beguiled
The heavy gait of night.—Sweet friends, to bed.—
A fortnight hold we this solemnity
In nightly revels and new jollity.   [*Exeunt.*

Enter PUCK.

PUCK.

> Now the hungry lion roars,
>   And the wolf behowls the moon;
> Whilst the heavy[3] ploughman snores,
>   All with weary task fordone.[4]
> Now the wasted brands do glow,
>   Whilst the screech-owl, screeching loud
> Puts the wretch that lies in woe
>   In remembrance of a shroud.
> Now it is the time of night,
>   That the graves, all gaping wide,
> Every one lets forth his sprite,
>   In the church-way paths to glide:
> And we fairies, that do run
>   By the triple Hecate's[5] team
> From the presence of the sun,
>   Following darkness like a dream,
> Now are frolic:[6] not a mouse
> Shall disturb this hallow'd house:
> I am sent, with broom, before,
> To sweep the dust behind the door.

---

[1] **overwatcht:** stayed up too late. [2] **palpable-gross:** palpably stupid.
[3] **heavy:** heavy with sleep. [4] **fordone:** exhausted. [5] **the triple Hecate:** thrice-crowned queen of night—Diana, Phoebe, and Hecate. [6] **frolic:** frolicsome; gay.

Enter OBERON *and* TITANIA, *with their* TRAIN.

OBERON.

Through the house give glimmering light,
   By the dead and drowsy fire;
Every elf and fairy sprite
   Hop as light as bird from brier;
And this ditty, after me,
Sing, and dance it trippingly.

TITANIA.

First, rehearse your song by rote,
To each word a warbling note:
Hand in hand, with fairy grace,
Will we sing, and bless this place.

                                        [*Song and dance.*

OBERON.

Now, until the break of day,
Through this house each fairy stray.
To the best bride-bed will we,
Which by us shall blessed be;[1]
And the issue there create
Ever shall be fortunate.
So shall all the couples three
Ever true in loving be;
And the blots[2] of Nature's hand
Shall not in their issue stand;
Never mole, hare-lip, nor scar,
Nor mark prodigious, such as are
Despised in nativity,[3]
Shall upon their children be.
With this field-dew consecrate,
Every fairy take his gait;[4]

---

[1] **shall blessed be:** a part of the marriage ceremony was the blessing of the bridal bed.
[2] **blots:** deformities.
[3] **nativity:** birth.
[4] **take his gait:** take his way.

And each several chamber bless,
Through this palace, with sweet peace:
Ever shall in safety rest,
And the owner of it blest.
    Trip away;
    Make no stay;
Meet me all by break of day.

> [*Exeunt* OBERON, TITANIA, *and* TRAIN.

PUCK.

If we shadows have offended,
Think but this, and all is mended,—
That you have but slumber'd here,
While these visions did appear.
And this weak and idle theme,
No more yielding but a dream,
Gentles, do not reprehend:[1]
If you pardon, we will mend.
And, as I am an honest Puck,
If we have unearned luck[2]
Now to 'scape the serpent's tongue,[3]
We will make amends ere long;
Else the Puck a liar call:
So, good night unto you all.
Give me your hands,[4] if we be friends,
And Robin shall restore amends.   [*Exit*

---

[1] reprehend: reprove us.
[2] If we have unearned luck: if we have better luck than we deserve.
[3] 'scape the serpent's tongue: escape being hissed at.
[4] your hands: applause.

William Shakespeare

TO THE READER

This Figure, that thou here seest put,
It was for gentle Shakespeare cut;
Wherein the Graver had a strife
With Nature, to out-do the life:
O, could he but have drawn his wit
As well in brass, as he hath hit
His face; the Print would then surpass
All, that was ever writ in brass.
But, since he cannot, Reader, look,
Not on his Picture, but his Book.

BEN: JONSON.

The Mediaeval view of man was generally not an exalted one. It saw him as more or less depraved, fallen from Grace as a result of Adam's sin; and the things of this world as of little value in terms of his salvation. Natural life was thought of mainly as a preparation for man's entry into Eternity. But Renaissance thought soon began to rehabilitate man and nature. Without denying man's need for Grace, men came gradually to accept the idea that there were "goods," values, "innocent delights" to be had in the world here and now. Man himself was seen no longer as wholly vile and depraved, incapable even of desiring goodness, but rather as Shakespeare saw him in *Hamlet*:

> *"What a piece of work is man! How noble in reason!*
> *how infinite in faculty! in form and moving how*
> *express and admirable! in action how like an angel!*
> *in apprehension how like a god! the beauty of the world!*
> *the paragon of animals!"*

It was, indeed, a very stirring time to be alive in. It was a time like spring, when promise, opportunity, challenge, and growth appeared where none had been dreamed of before. Perhaps this is why there is so much poetry of springtime in the age of Shakespeare.

Edited with Introduction and Suggestions for Study by Dr. David G. Pitt

Notes Edited by Lucy Mabry Fitzpatrick

AN AIRMONT CLASSIC
Published by Airmont Publishing Co., Inc.